HIGH IMPACT PUBLIC SPEAKING

WILLIAM T. BROOKS

Prentice Hall, Englewood Cliffs, New Jersey 07632

Library of Congress Cataloging-in-Publication Data

Brooks, William T.
  High impact public speaking.

  Includes index.
  1. Public speaking. 2. Oral communication. I. Title.
PN4121.B7245   1988   808.5'1   87-17580
ISBN 0-13-387655-1

The publisher offers discounts on this book when ordered in bulk quantities. For more information, write:

    Special Sales/College Marketing
    Prentice-Hall, Inc.
    College Technical and Reference Division
    Englewood Cliffs, NJ 07632

Editorial/production supervision and
  interior design: Sylvia Moore
Cover and Jacket design: Lundgren Graphics, Ltd.
Manufacturing buyer: Lorraine Fumoso

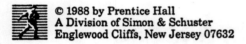 © 1988 by Prentice Hall
A Division of Simon & Schuster
Englewood Cliffs, New Jersey 07632

All rights reserved. No part of this book may be
reproduced, in any form or by any means,
without permission in writing from the publisher.

Printed in the United States of America

10 9 8 7 6 5 4 3 2 1

ISBN 0-13-387655-1 01

Prentice-Hall International (UK) Limited, *London*
Prentice-Hall of Australia Pty. Limited, *Sydney*
Prentice-Hall Canada Inc., *Toronto*
Prentice-Hall Hispanoamericana, S.A., *Mexico*
Prentice-Hall of India Private Limited, *New Delhi*
Prentice-Hall of Japan, Inc., *Tokyo*
Simon & Schuster Asia Pte. Ltd., *Singapore*
Editora Prentice-Hall do Brasil, Ltda., *Rio de Janeiro*

This book is gratefully and humbly dedicated to Mr. Harry Bolich, retired from the Department of Speech, Gettysburg College.

It is my hope that this work will help to repay a talented teacher for his many years of work and selfless dedication.

CONTENTS

PREFACE

**PART I   GAINING FAVOR
          AS A PUBLIC SPEAKER**   **1**

INTRODUCTION   **1**

    A Brief Overview   **3**
    The Master Key to High Personal
       and Professional Impact   **4**
    A High Impact Speech Is Effective   **5**
    A High Impact Speech F.I.T.S.   **6**

1   YOU START BY SPEAKING   **9**

    Why Experience Really Is the Best Teacher   **11**
    How Practice Can Make You
       Consistently Good   **15**
    How to Practice Most Productively   **19**
    So, What Have We Said?   **22**
    Action Steps   **23**

2   CONQUERING STAGE FRIGHT   **25**

    Scared Stiff   **27**
    What Is Stage Fright?   **27**
    What Causes Stage Fright?   **29**

How to Make All Your Butterflies Fly
   in Formation   32
So, What Have We Said?   37
Action Steps   38

3 HOW TO GET STARTED WITH A BANG   39

Make Every Speech an Event   41
What a Good Opening Can Do for You   41
Come on Strong from the Start   42
So, What Have We Said?   50
Action Steps   51

4 GIVE 'EM A SHOW THEY'LL NEVER FORGET   53

In Search of High Impact   55
How to Give 'Em All You Are   57
Perform with Power   60
So, What Have We Said?   66
Action Steps   67

PART II   CREATING INTEREST   69

5 HOW TO HOLD AN AUDIENCE IN THE PALM OF YOUR HAND   69

Now That I Have Your Attention...   71
How to Make People Want to Hear
   Your Ideas   71
How to Move From Favor to Response   77
How to Keep Them Begging for More   80
So, What Have We Said?   81
Action Steps   81

6 HOW TO HOLD INTEREST — 83

May I Have Your Attention, Please? 85
Utilize All Your Speaking Skills 85
Deal Effectively with Distractions
 and Interruptions 90
So, What Have We Said? 96
Action Steps 96

PART III CONVEYING A THOUGHT — 97

7 STARTING AT THE BACK END —WITH RESULTS — 97

Making the Most of Prime Time 99
Asking the Most Crucial,
 But Least Asked, Question 100
Making Your Message Fit
 Your Audience's Purpose 102
Pulling It All Together into
 a Clearly Targeted Message 105
So, What Have We Said? 109
Action Steps 110

8 HOW TO PREPARE A POWERFUL SPEECH — 111

Saying What You Want to Say
 with Impact 113
Gathering All the Materials You Need 113
Organizing Your Speech
 for Maximum Impact 116
Planning for a Powerful Close 120
So, What Have We Said? 123
Action Steps 123

9 HOW TO PRESENT YOUR IDEAS WITH MORE POWER   125

Power Comes from Clarity and Persuasion   127
How to Make Your Audience Understand What You Mean   127
Flip Charts Can Liven Up Your Presentations   132
How to Make People Care Enough to Act   134
So, What Have We Said?   136
Action Steps   136

PART IV   SCORING   137

10   GETTING WHAT YOU CAME AFTER   137

How Good Are You, Really?   139
How to Get Good Feedback During Your Speech   139
How to Get Useful Feedback After the Speech   140
Strategies for Getting Feedback   140
How Always to Make Your Next Speech Your Best One   142
So, What Have We Said?   143
It Is Results That Count   144
If I May Say in Closing...   144

PREFACE

Your success in life will probably be in direct proportion to your ability to communicate your ideas, concerns, and dreams to other people, often through speaking to groups. If you do it well, public speaking looks easy; but if you do it poorly, you have big problems. For that reason, many otherwise very capable and confident people

- feel their blood run cold when asked to make a public report or presentation.
- pass up opportunities for professional growth.
- muddle along with mediocre performances
- avoid getting involved in community projects, even though they care deeply about their goals

In fact, speaking before a group is the foremost fear of the typical American, according to *The Book of Lists,* ranking above the fear of flying and even the fear of death.

Yet for all the awe and mystery that surrounds it, public speaking is simple, easy to learn, and extremely rewarding once you understand the basic principles. Unfortunately, most of the books on the subject are either so technical or so academic that they confuse and frighten away more people than they help.

I chose to write this book as a direct response to requests from my clients and from people who make up the audiences of my more than 200 fee-paid speeches and seminars each year. Again and again, people have asked for a simple, down-to-earth guide to public speaking for managers, salespeople, community leaders, and other professionals who want to learn to speak well but do not want to make a career of it.

Practical Ideas Based On Sound Principles

High-Impact Public Speaking offers practical ideas and useful techniques that were forged in the crucible of my own life. They have to do with such topics as how to conquer stage fright, how to get people to listen to you, and how to make people care about what you say.

Every suggestion you will read in this book is based on personal experiences and has been tested and proven before many audiences. These suggestions offer more than ideas which have worked for one person; they are based on sound principles which have stood the test of centuries and have proved useful to many of the greatest speakers the world has known. I have studied the works of the masters and have had opportunities to learn firsthand from top professional speakers.

This book of practical ideas and techniques based on sound principles can save you time if you adapt it to your own needs, while you save face and avoid embarrassment by learning from our mistakes.

You Can Do It, If...

If you have been able to read the simple, plain talk I have used so far, you can learn everything you need to know to make you a public speaker. Nothing in this book will be more complicated than what you have already read.

"You can't teach a person anything," said the wise Galileo, "you can only help him discover it for himself." That has been the guiding principle I have used in writing this book. I will share with you my ideas and experiences, and you will test those ideas and adapt them to your own speaking style and situation.

What you gain from this book will be in direct proportion to how willing you are to search, to make your own discoveries, and to practice what you learn. It does not matter how little or how much experience you have had, what failures you may have experienced, what others may have said to you about your abilities and shortcomings as a speaker, or what expectations others have for you. All that really matters is how much of yourself you are willing to invest.

When You Care Enough

A young musician once approached an internationally renowned concert pianist and asked, "Sir, how much time do you practice each day?"

"I spend eight hours every day in practice . . . not one minute less," said the old maestro.

"But why?" asked the novice. "Why do you practice so much when you are so good?"

"I wish to become superb!" came the simple reply.

Maybe you're not ready even to think about becoming "superb" yet. Maybe all you want to do at this stage is to learn how to stand in front of a group without feeling like you're going to have a nervous breakdown.

Remember:

- Oral Roberts, as a young man, stammered so badly that his friends openly ridiculed him. Regardless of how you feel about his theology, you must admit he has done well as a public speaker.
- Demosthenes was considered the greatest orator of ancient Greece in the "Golden Age of Oratory." But his first attempt was so poor that the audience booed him off the stage.

Whatever your present level of competence, that's where we'll start. How far you go depends upon how seriously you take what you read, and how much of yourself you choose to invest.

Let's get down to business!

INTRODUCTION

PURPOSE

What gives a speech high impact? Perhaps an even more appropriate question for you is, how can this book enable you to become a high impact public speaker? Those are questions you will find answered in this section as we explore:

1. what is impact
2. the master key to high impact public speaking
3. how this book can help you become an effective speaker

"Let thy speech be better than silence, or be silent."

—*Dionysius*

A BRIEF OVERVIEW

Some people have a knack for getting others to help them do things that matter to them.

- John F. Kennedy inspired a whole generation to forge a new and more vigorous way of thinking and acting.
- Ronald Reagan rallied a confused nation to meet the new challenge he defined.
- Winston Churchill held a dispirited people together to combat one of the greatest threats of international tyranny the world had ever faced.

Why? What was it that enabled them to gain such a widespread support and enthusiasm for their ideas?

Magic, Mania Or Mastery?

Some people would attribute it to that intangible quality called *charisma,* which the dictionary defines as "a personal magic of leadership." To them, such a person is gifted with almost superhuman powers and abilities to influence people.

Others would say that great leaders are the product of their times—that they see which way the parade is heading and run faster than anyone else to get in front. The American Revolution, according to such reasoning, was an idea whose time had come, and George Washington just happened to have the right ideas at the right time.

I would suggest that such outstanding leadership in any arena comes neither from the magic of an inborn gift nor the ability to predict the fads and manias of the masses. Rather, leading others to high achievement comes from a mastery of the basic skills of communicating effectively.

What It Is, Is Impact!

A principle of leadership called *impact management* recognizes that in our society leaders are judged by their impact. For example, most political candidates are surrounded by make-up artists, speech writers, and coaches who help them achieve the maximum impact for every speech and action. In the business world, who gets the promotion? Frequently, it is not the brightest or most capable candidate.

Often, the people who get ahead in business are those who have the most impact on the decision makers, and on those who work with them, under them, and within their fields. Many of them are also able to influence people in their communities.

THE MASTER KEY TO HIGH PERSONAL AND PROFESSIONAL IMPACT

Essentially, what gives leaders great personal and professional impact is the ability to communicate effectively their ideas, their dreams, and concerns to those who can do something about them.

For example:

- Thomas A. Edison was known for his ability to use laboratory assistants to help him sort through the necessary experiments that led to his great discoveries. He could communicate to them what he was hoping to find and inspire them to explore with him.
- Albert Einstein once said, "The whole of science is nothing more than a refinement of everyday thinking." Few people ever contributed more to that dialogue on "everyday thinking."
- Henry Ford's impact came not so much from his invention of an automobile (many others invented fine automobiles), nor even from his ingenious idea of an assembly line. His real impact came from his unique ability to get other people to do things.

Today, the people who have high impact are those who know how to communicate effectively with others, to win their loyalty, and to influence them to do things.

What this means to you is:

1. Your personal and professional progress are dependent upon the impact you have on others.
2. Your impact will be largely dependent upon your ability to communicate effectively with the important people in your life.

The focus of this book is on one of the most vital tools for communicating effectively—public speaking. My goal is to show you how to make people listen to you, how to make them understand your meaning, how to make them care, and how to influence them to act.

I want to help you discover how to use your own personality and abilities to make a powerful impact with every speech. I want to share with you some high-impact ideas and techniques that are equally effective whether the purpose of your speech is to inform, to motivate, to inspire, or merely to entertain.

A HIGH-IMPACT SPEECH IS EFFECTIVE

Simply stated, a high impact speech is one that is effective. My dictionary gives three definitions of "effective":

1. Strikingly impressive
2. Capable of producing a desired outcome
3. Ready for service or action

When you combine those three concepts, you get what I call a high impact speech—one that is strikingly impressive, capable of producing a desired outcome, and able to prime the audience for service or action.

The speaker—not the content—is the most vital element of a speech. The single most important ingredient of a speech is the delivery and the appropriate impact to meet the situation.

This idea departs sharply from most technical and academic books on public speaking which state that content is the primary concern with the speaker's delivery only a secondary consideration. However, after more than 20 years of public speaking, I can tell you that effective speaking has more to do with emotions than with technical perfection or logic. Perhaps Marshall McCluhan expressed it best when he said "The medium is the message."

Effective Speaking Versus Oratory

Two men spoke in the same small Pennsylvania town on November 19, 1863. The occasion was the dedication of a national cemetery.

The first speaker was Edward Everett. Everett was considered a genius. He studied at Harvard (graduating at age 17) and abroad, and had an extraordinary memory. He is listed in encyclopedias as one of the greatest orators of the nineteenth century. He had arrived in town several days before he was to give the speech, to study the people and prepare his speech. As he stepped to the platform, a hush fell across the audience. His powerful material, carefully organized remarks, and eloquent oratory held the attention of his audience for more than an hour.

There was another speaker in the little Pennsylvania town that day, a man so awkward in appearance that one of his critics called him "that big baboon." Due to the press of his duties, he had had little time to prepare. He had only jotted down a few notes (some historians say on a napkin) on the brief train ride from Washington that day. When he strolled to the podium, he had no smile for the audience, no humorous stories, no heart-warming illustrations. His speech contained only 266 words and lasted less than five minutes.

"Fourscore and seven years ago..." he started, and the rest is so familiar that most fifth-grade students in America can recite it for you. As I am sure you have guessed, the second speaker was Abraham Lincoln, and his message was the famous Gettysburg Address.

His speech touched the hearts of the people; it spoke to their needs, their dreams, their fears, their sufferings. When he had finished, there wasn't a dry eye in the audience—including the eyes of the first speaker.

A HIGH IMPACT SPEECH F.I.T.S.

The most crucial factor in making a high-impact speech is that the speech fits the speaker, the audience, its purpose, and the occasion. To borrow a phrase from Mr. Lincoln, his speech at Gettysburg was "altogether fitting and proper." That, essentially, is what high-impact public speaking is all about.

The ancient Greeks, who developed public speaking to a new high, gave us three words that can help to put it all in perspective. The words are:

- *ethos*, which suggests that an audience buys you as a speaker, and is willing to hear what you say
- *pathos*, which means the audience makes an emotional commitment to you and your ideas
- *logos*, which has to do with the content and meaning of your message

It is only after you have sold yourself to your audience (ethos) and gained an emotional commitment (pathos) from them, that you can concern yourself with the content and meaning (logos) of your message—as vital as that message and meaning may be.

In modern language, what we are really talking about is gaining *favor*, creating *interest*, and conveying a *thought*. When you have accomplished this, your speech will score.

An acronym of the first letters of those four key words is a formula for high-impact public speaking.

F - Favor
I - Interest
T - Thought
S - Score

The F.I.T.S. formula is a simple and convenient way of exploring the key ingredients of creating high impact in public speaking. Each element is considered as a complete step. *Step 1: Gaining Favor* shows how to gain the favor of your audience and how to capture their attention. *Step 2: Creating Interest* focuses on getting people to listen and care about what you have to say. *Step 3: Conveying a Thought* offers guidelines to building a clear and readily understandable speech. *Step 4: Scoring* shows how to always get the results you desire.

In all, you will find this to be a fresh and exciting departure from the stodgy, ineffective approach of investing most of your energies on the content instead of your delivery. If you will take it seriously, you can become a high-impact public speaker, and your audiences will be forever grateful.

Eloquence Versus Impact

Edward Everett was often called an eloquent speaker. His ideas were arranged with the logic of a philosopher, his words were chosen with the precision of a surgeon and spoken with the fervor of an evangelist, and his technical speaking skills would match the skills of a master architect.

Yet, as one of his critics observed: "When you hear him, you button your coat to keep from taking a cold."

But Abe Lincoln warmed the hearts of a troubled nation with the sheer impact of his personality and emotional involvement with his audiences.

Or consider the success of President Ronald Reagan against political opponents. His ability to speak with impact is what has carried him into the forefront of government. He appropriately reads the audience, communicates well, has a good image and a sense of humor, and he does not try to convey too many ideas at once. Certainly, he violates many of the rules of oratory: He stumbles over words, sometimes gets confused, and frequently makes bloopers. Yet he is called the great communicator, and he is.

Candidate Ronald Reagan spoke with much stronger impact than Jimmy Carter in the 1980 election and that carried him to a landslide victory. In 1984, he crushed Fritz Mondale, who just did not have the impact.

In a contest of eloquence versus impact, impact always wins.

How High Impact Can Enhance Your Career

The principles and ideas you will discover in what follows really work.

For example, about six years ago, I was invited to do a speech for the Chevrolet Division of General Motors. It was the first time they had ever used an outside speaker for one of their major retailing schools, and I was hoping that speech would open a door for me to do additional work with Chevrolet.

As you might guess, the sales managers and program chairpersons were very demanding. As one of 15 top professional speakers, I had been previewed three times before the invitation had been given. The pressure was high. By using the principles of the F.I.T.S. formula for high-impact public speaking, I came out as the top-rated speaker, and I have been working with Chevrolet as a consultant and trainer ever since.

Moreover, my success with that one major corporation has opened countless doors for me. I have had the opportunity to test my principles and ideas in a wide variety of speaking situations, and found that they always work.

The Chevrolet program involved about 20 people in a seminar or workshop program. I have also spoken at large, enthusiastic rallies which really tested my public-speaking skills. I have held sessions with presidents of major corporations, where we rolled up our sleeves and worked through problems together. The requirements for each of those situations were unique, but the same basic techniques have proved successful in all formats. Success in the corporate world is a direct result of how effectively you speak before a group and how much impact you have.

Whether or not it is your goal to become a professional speaker, if you are ready to discover the awesome power of high personal and professional impact through the F.I.T.S. system of public speaking, let us begin.

1
YOU START BY SPEAKING

PURPOSE

Your first task when you step before an audience is to sell yourself. Step 1 focuses on how to gain the favor of your audience by conquering your stage fright, getting started with a bang, and giving your audience a show they will never forget. In this chapter, you will discover:

1. why experience really is the best teacher
2. how practice can make you consistently good
3. how to practice most productively

"Practice and thought might gradually forge many an art."

—*Virgil*

One of the toughest speaking assignments I ever drew was doing a four-hour seminar during a rally for 1,200 people. Holding the attention of such a large audience for such a long time was enough of a challenge to test everything I had ever learned about public speaking. The real clincher was that the next speaker to follow me on the program was Dr. Norman Vincent Peale, a man whose name is literally a household word around the world.

Obviously, people were not too interested or enthused about hearing me, particularly since Dr. Peale was going to talk for about 45 minutes, while I had a four-hour seminar to conduct. Yet that seminar program, in my opinion, was a very strong performance as shown in my strong evaluations from the audience and program planners.

One reason I was able to do so well was that I responded positively to all the pressure. More important, I responded positively because I had done virtually thousands of professional speeches prior to this one. In fact, I had given more than 600 free speeches before I started as a professional speaker. Absolutely nothing can help you develop your speaking skills more quickly or effectively than experience.

WHY EXPERIENCE REALLY IS THE BEST TEACHER

The only way you will ever improve at speaking is to speak. That may sound simplistic, but it's true. You can study all the available material and get an intellectual understanding of the mechanics of speaking, but the only way to really develop your speaking skills is to get out there and do it.

It's a little like selling. You can study sales theory, get personal coaching from a skilled trainer, and become thoroughly familiar with the product you are to sell. But you'll never know what selling is all about until you have to talk face to face with a real live prospect.

Why is experience so crucial to learning how to speak with high impact? Let's explore six very good reasons.

Experience Gives You Instant Feedback

One thing you learn quickly in the game of speaking is that you get some valuable feedback on the way you say and do things. It's true that most audiences tend at least to be courteous in expressing their feelings, but they do react immediately.

It does not take long, for example, to learn when applause is enthusiastic and when it is merely courteous, or to learn the difference between a ripple of polite laughter and uproarious belly laughs. Some audiences will be quite open about how they feel and what they think. If you can keep your cool and risk your ego, such groups can help you make some very helpful discoveries.

Some of the most valuable lessons I ever learned about speaking came from the feedback I received from groups of potential investors during my early days of selling. The firm I was working for would hold meetings, sometimes three a day, for people who wanted to invest. I didn't know much about investments, but I had done a lot of speaking so I was usually the person making the presentations.

Talk about antagonistic audiences! Those were people who felt that someone was trying to get into their pockets, and they resisted. They expressed themselves very vocally about everything I said and did. At the time, it was hard to take, but in looking back on it, that was probably some of the best training I have ever had.

Later, we devote a whole chapter to how to get informative feedback and what to do with it. For now, let me simply say that one thing you always do with feedback is to recognize its value as a way of learning.

YOU DISCOVER WHAT WORKS FOR YOU

Experience alone can teach you what works well for you and what works well in certain situations. You will soon develop a repertoire of techniques and stories you enjoy using, but it's only as you use them again and again that you will develop the skills to use them well, and the wisdom to know when to use them.

For example, an organization which sponsors programs for corporate presidents asked me to do a program for about 60 company presidents. Each one of the chief executives was in charge of a company that exceeded $50 million in annual sales volume. I was dealing with a topic on productivity in management.

My company is very small, and I could work for 20 years and never make $50 million. There was a time in my life when speaking to such an august group would have intimidated me, even though I knew I had something worthwhile to say. But experience had taught me a trick or two. I took control of the situation early. They knew that I was an entrepreneur, so I played on that aspect. The session went very well, and I believe it was because I had been in similar situations before and knew exactly what would work.

Let's stop for just a moment and take a look at some of the performances I have mentioned. One was for a group of 20 Chevrolet sales managers, another was for a rally of 1200 sales people, and still another was for a group of 60 company presidents. Each of those programs required a different set of skills, which I had developed through years of doing all kinds of programs.

YOU DISCOVER WHAT DOESN'T WORK FOR YOU

You read an exciting story, or watch a humorist tell a great joke, and you decide that's a sure winner. But the first time you use it, it bombs! No matter how many times you try it, it drops to the floor with a thud.

Through trial and error, you learn that there are some things that just don't work for you. They may be right for someone else, but there is something about your personality that makes it impossible for you to get a good response when using them. So you learn to abandon what experiences teach you do not work for you.

Experience Forces You To Improve

Experience forces you to improve. If you have any ego at all, it simply cannot stand flopping every time you speak, so it will drive you to get better and better.

While some things you read may sound trite, it's only through experience that you learn why so many writers mention them. For example, you may read that exceeding your allotted time is one of the cardinal sins of a public speaker. You may feel that's an exaggeration, but if a couple of audiences get up and walk out on you, you'll learn the hard way that you simply cannot get away with it.

Experience Helps You Develop Your Own Style

For years, I would subconsciously try to mimic the styles of other speakers. But I never really felt comfortable trying to be like other people, and my audiences seemed to prefer hearing the real speakers instead of hearing my imitation of them. After ten years of doing this, I began to discover that each of us can only be our best when we are truly ourselves. Gradually, I settled into my own style. Now I'm very comfortable with that style and, when I've done a program, I know very well that it was Bill Brooks who spoke to those people, not someone else.

Interestingly, my audience responses and evaluations have

greatly improved as I have become more and more the real Bill Brooks. It's not that I am the greatest speaker in the world, but now I am the greatest speaker Bill Brooks can be at this stage of development.

As hard as it may be for you to believe, you can only be your best when you are truly your own person, with your own unique style. It's the greatest thing you have going for you! You can only discover and develop your own style as you give enough talks to get to know who you really are when you stand before a group.

Experience Builds Confidence

Public speaking is like most other activities in life—the more you do it, the more confident you become. If confidence comes from success, it's important to find a few things you can do very well and do them often enough so that you can do them almost automatically.

I learned this when I was coaching college football. If my team was facing a big game and I put too many new plays into the game plan, we would lose. Thus I learned from experience to stick to what our team knew best and build around our greatest strengths. We consistently won because at no time would you ever find more than 10 percent of the plays in our game plan to be new.

As you hold to what has worked well for you as a speaker and do it often enough, you will slowly become more and more confident. There will be enough time for learning new tricks as you gain the experience which only the years can teach. If you will always use 90 percent tested and proven materials in each speech with never more than 10 percent new material, you'll be amazed at how quickly your confidence level will build.

Experience Creates Desire

An old saying from the printing industry claims that "Once you get printer's ink in your blood, you'll never be able to get it out."

The equivalent could be said, and even magnified, for public speaking. All you need is a few great successes at speaking, and you will find yourself hopelessly hooked for life. There's something about standing before an audience and having them respond warmly to you that creates an overpowering desire to keep doing it, and to do it better and better.

Experience Gives You Exposure

As I mentioned earlier, my first successful speech for Chevrolet opened many doors for me. But it didn't start there!

Even when I was doing free speeches, I found that people who heard me would invite me to speak to other groups. It wasn't long before I was booked for all the spare time I had. I've discovered that the same thing has happened to countless other speakers. You would be surprised at how few people are willing to invest the time and creative energy needed to learn how to give an interesting speech. When word gets around that you are worth hearing, you will be amazed at how many invitations you'll get.

Another interesting thing happens as you start getting more exposure as a speaker, even in situations that seem far removed from your career. Word has a way of getting around within your own company. You will find yourself being repeatedly pushed to the forefront as your peers and superiors discover that you can handle leadership responsibilities. I know of nothing that can enhance your professional standing more quickly than gaining a reputation as a good public speaker, regardless of what your profession may be.

HOW PRACTICE CAN MAKE YOU CONSISTENTLY GOOD

They say that "practice makes perfect," but I doubt it.

A reporter asked the world-famous pianist, Arthur Rubinstein, near the end of his life, "Are you the greatest musician who ever lived, as some people have said?"

"Music is an art, not a science," said the wise old maestro, "and no one ever becomes the greatest at an art—they could always be greater!" The same could be said about the art of public speaking.

No, practice will not make you perfect, but what it can do is make you consistently good, and sometimes great.

Perhaps you have noticed that not all practice is equally helpful. Actually, some forms of practice can be harmful by reinforcing bad habits as effectively as they reinforce good habits. However, let's look at some practice techniques that can make you consistently good.

Practice Putting A Smile In Your Voice

You'll be amazed at how disarming it is to your audience for you to speak with a smile in your voice. Smiles come through much more than you might realize. With a little practice, you can close your eyes while you are listening to a speaker and tell instantly when he or she is smiling. It shows up as a cheerful and reassuring tone, a softness in voice, and a feeling of warmth.

A smiling voice helps your audience relax and let down their guard. Thus, it helps you make even the most controversial points and remarks with a minimum of resistance. Yet, most novice speakers get so caught up in the content of what they are saying that they sound (and look) as serious as a cardiac arrest.

Try reading a few paragraphs into a recorder making a conscious effort not to smile. Then read the same passage into the recorder while making a conscious effort to smile. Listen back and see if you can tell the difference. You'll probably like your smiling voice a lot better, and so will your audience.

Whatever other techniques you may learn about public speaking, none will ever serve you better than a smiling face and voice.

Practice Movements And Facial Expressions

Comedian Bill Cosby has remained one of the top performers in America for decades, largely because he draws his audiences so completely into his routines. His most effective technique for doing that is the masterful way he uses his face and body to convey feelings.

So crucial are those gestures and expressions that he is always looking for new ways to enable the audience to really see them. His latest device is to use a giant television screen as a backdrop while performing for the huge audiences he now draws. What's on the gigantic screen in living color? You guessed it—a close-up shot of his hands and face!

The skill of expression is a powerful technique which you can also master with enough practice. Try speaking in front of a mirror and try to convey more with your face and gestures than you do with your voice. If you are trying to convey surprise, look surprised; if you are conveying amusement, look amused. Whatever you want that audience to feel, make them see it in your face and hands.

Practice Vocalizing

A good speaking voice is almost unnoticeable because it does its job so well. When people focus more on your delivery than on your message, your voice has become the star—not you.

Here are some pointers to help you practice productively the high art of vocalizing:

- Practice proper volume level. If you speak too loudly, you'll blow your audience away; too softly, and they can't hear you. Develop a pleasing volume level.
- Practice proper pitch. Using a monotone will put people to sleep, but too many variations make you sound like a fake. Find the right balance, and work on using a variety of pitches which can make you more pleasant to hear.
- Practice quality. Tense muscles and vocal chords make your voice sound thin, but a clear, full, mellow, and enthusiastic voice enables you to gain acceptance and be heard.
- Practice enunciation. Holding your head down, mumbling and not articulating clearly can destroy your effectiveness as a speaker. Practice holding your head up, speaking clearly and distinctly, and saying every word in such a way that it can be heard and understood.
- Practice pacing. Some speakers spout out words like a machine gun, while others drag along. Either can be very distracting. Learn to pace your speaking to fit your audience, and to vary your pace for emphasis.
- Practice inflection. A skilled speaker may use as many as 25 different notes to convey a variety of meanings. By practicing your inflections, you can greatly improve your speaking voice.

Remember, your voice identifies you as unique in all the world. It is one of your most important tools. So, what kind of voice do you have?

Is it friendly? Is it pleasing to the ears?
Is it natural? Does it sound real?
Is it forceful? Does your voice convey power and energy?
Is it expressive? Can you convey your emotions through your voice?
Is it understandable? Can everyone hear you clearly, without feeling shouted at?

Through proper practice and exercise you can develop a more effective speaking voice, which can give you much more impact as a speaker.

Practice Telling Stories

Think about one of the best speeches you have ever heard, and notice what you remember about it. You might not even remember the speaker's main points, but chances are good that you can remember at least one or two stories he or she told.

Successful speakers—the ones who are perennial favorites— use a lot of stories. They know that stories make listening more fun, help people understand complex ideas more clearly, and are easily remembered.

There is a definite art to telling stories. Maybe that's why an old pro like Dr. Norman Vincent Peale is so popular year after year. He is a master storyteller. As you listen to him spin a yarn, you feel as if you are actually a part of the action. You can feel the emotions of the characters, sense their dangers and conflicts, and savor their victories.

As with any art, powerful storytelling requires a lot of practice. One outstanding professional speaker says he never tells a story to an audience until he has practiced it at least ten times alone.

When you are practicing telling stories, ask yourself some prodding questions:

1. Can my audience feel what the characters felt?
2. Can my audience identify with my characters?
3. Can my audience sense the mood of the story from the first line?
4. Can my audience see themselves as characters in my story?
5. Can I always remember precisely every detail of the story as I want to tell it?

The more you practice productively telling stories, the more impact you will have as a speaker.

Practice Humor

People who can get an audience to laugh heartily with them are always in demand as speakers. Yet, for all its power, few public speakers ever develop their skills at using this excellent tool.

Humor seems to come so naturally to some people that they can make you laugh at almost anything. Unfortunately, many of those who have the potential to become great humorists invest so much energy in finding new material that they do not practice their jokes and cracks enough to become as funny as they could be. Others have such a hard time with humor that they avoid it by saying something like, "I'm just not cut out to be a comedian."

Whatever your speaking style, subject area, and personality are like, remember that anyone—including you—can use humor to advantage. And no matter how effectively you use humor, you can always get more mileage from it by practicing it more vigorously.

Try practicing the worst joke you ever heard, until you can tell it and make it funny.

Study what kinds of jokes and one-liners get the best responses and analyze why.

Study your failures and see if you can figure out why they don't go over.

Make a list of your ten best humorous stories and practice telling them.

Practice setting up a joke or crack for maximum impact.

Spend at least five times as much time practicing the humor you already use as you do looking for new humor.

One of the great fallacies about humor is that if a story has been heard, it won't go over. A good joke, told by a skillful speaker, will be funny to most people no matter how many times it has been told. Conversely, the latest joke, if poorly told, will not be funny no matter how few people have heard it.

Whether you have a keen sense of humor and ready wit or are as dry as last year's corn shucks, you can use humor to great advantage if you are willing to practice enough to make it work for you.

HOW TO PRACTICE MOST PRODUCTIVELY

For all its popularity, self-watching is a notoriously limited way to improve your speaking skills. Have you ever noticed, for example, that you cannot really see your own eyes in a mirror? Even if you are looking straight at them, you can only focus on one of them at a time. If you glance at your chin, you lose sight of your eyes. Our eyes are designed to focus on one tiny point. Symbolically, that's the way it is with all efforts at self-watching.

So, constantly analyzing yourself, or simply saying your speech over and over again, is seldom very helpful. It is better to get help and to use more productive aids in practicing. Let's look at a few ways you can practice more productively.

Seek Constructive Criticism

"People ask you for criticism, but they only want praise," said Somerset Maugham in his monumental work, *Of Human Bondage*. He's right, you know! Real improvement only comes when we can lay aside our need to be reaffirmed and seek out truly helpful criticism. However, when I suggest you seek out constructive criticism, I am not talking about catty remarks or biting barbs hurled at you by people who may be jealous of your success. While it is possible to learn even from such small-minded people, unless your ego is invincible, the best thing you can do is ignore petty criticisms.

What I'm suggesting is that you seek out competent people who will offer suggestions as to ways you can improve your speaking skills. It is even better if you can have skilled speakers listen to you and offer tips on ways to improve. You'll find many such people at Toastmasters, International. That fine organization is made up of people who have a sincere interest in improving themselves and the art of speaking. It is one of the best ways I know to gain insights as to when you're good or when you're bad, and to get valuable feedback.

Whether you join Toastmasters (which I highly recommend) or look for constructive critics elsewhere, the important thing is not to be overly critical of yourself, but always to look for ways to improve your speaking. Forget about perfection. What you strive for is that consistency which only comes as you get feedback and start to implement all of these various lessons.

One caution about critics: Even the best of them can fall into the trap of trying to impose their style on you. Listen to their suggestions, but guard your own style. One good way to do that is to compare the criticisms of several skilled speakers before you make any significant change.

Record, Review, And Compare

One of the most useful, yet underutilized, tools for self-evaluation is the simple cassette recorder. For some reason, most of us shy away from that monster and hate to hear a recording of ourselves.

But if you really want to learn to speak, here's a very helpful technique. Record all your practice sessions and review them several times while looking for specific flaws and strong points.

For example, if you notice you have a habit of saying "you know," or "uhhh," you can listen to see just how big a problem it is. Or, you can check to see how good your diction is. I always tell novice speakers, "If you can make it on a dead tape recorder, you can make it anywhere."

Another helpful technique is to save some of your better practice tapes and compare them with tapes you make some time later. You can chart your progress and it's a great way to boost your confidence!

You might even want to invest in a videotape camera and

player. But watch out! That will show up every flaw! I recommend that beginners stay away from video until they get some experience and confidence. There are two big reasons.

First, comparing yourself to network quality images is always a losing game. Professional cameras and cameramen, makeup, and lighting can do wonders for a network personality. Your home system will always make you look bad when compared to them.

Second, the techniques for speaking well on television are quite different from those required for performing before an audience. But, if you understand the limits, and your self-confidence can stand it, you can learn a lot from videotapes. Until that time, I suggest you stick with the audio-cassette recorder.

Write Down Criticisms And Work On Them

"The palest ink is greater than the strongest memory," the ancient Orientals used to say. We know they used to say it, because someone wrote it down.

As you get constructive criticism and practice with a cassette recorder, make notes about your diction, delivery, and other important elements. Periodically, make a list of the top priorities on your "to improve" list, and concentrate mostly on them.

Some speakers find it helpful to keep a brief critique of all their speaking experiences and store them in a notebook. By checking back from time to time, you can spot areas where you are improving and, perhaps more important, areas in which you are still making the same mistakes.

However you do it, writing down your criticisms gives you very specific ideas of what to work on.

Watch Speakers You Admire

One of the best ways to become successful at any activity is to watch the people who are already successful. It's helpful to watch everything they do and the way they do everything. You can be sure that if they are really good, nothing they do is accidental. And you can often learn by simple observation what it took them years to learn.

However, there are some dangers in watching speakers you admire. First, you can become so preoccupied with comparing yourself with them that you miss anything helpful you could learn. Comparing yourself with others is always a losing game. You will either become an insufferable egotist or develop an inferiority complex. Leave that game to the hopelessly insecure.

Second, you can fall into the trap I fell into of trying to copy them. You do not have to become like someone else to learn from them. In fact, you can never be the same as someone else no matter how hard you try. Fortunately, your uniqueness is the best thing you have going for you!

Third, by watching top-notch speakers too much, you can lose touch with the differences in their audiences and yours. For example, Don Rickles has made a fortune by cutting people to shreds in nightclubs and on television. But if you try making a fool of your boss at a company sales meeting, you might find yourself looking for a job. Always keep in mind that every audience is unique, and what works well in one setting might create trouble in another.

SO, WHAT HAVE WE SAID?

The first step in becoming a high-impact speaker is to gain the favor of your audience, and the best starting place for doing that is to get as much experience as you can.

Experience really is the best teacher because it:

1. gives you instant feedback on how well you are doing and where you need to improve
2. forces you to improve
3. helps you develop your own style
4. builds your self-confidence
5. creates the desire to improve
6. gives you the exposure you need to make contacts

We have also seen that practice can make you consistently good, but that some types of practice are more helpful than others. To get the most mileage out of your practice:

1. Practice putting a smile in your voice.
2. Practice your movements and facial expressions.
3. Practice using your voice to maximum advantage.
4. Practice telling stories.
5. Practice using humor.

Finally, some pointers on how to practice most productively are:

1. Value and seek constructive criticism.
2. Record, review, and compare your progress.

3. Write down criticisms and work on them.
4. Watch speakers you admire.

This has been a long chapter, but it's a long road to becoming all you can be as a high-impact speaker. I hope you'll join me.

ACTION STEPS

1. Make a copy of the summary and keep it handy for ready reference.
2. Plan a strategy and set goals for implementing in your own life each of the concepts discussed in this chapter.

CONQUERING STAGE FRIGHT

PURPOSE

The first priority in becoming a high-impact public speaker is gaining the favor of your audience, and the first step in gaining that favor is to get as much experience as you can. Before they can take that first step, many people have to find a way to stop their knees from bumping together. The fact is that most people are scared stiff of standing in front of a group. In this chapter, you will discover:

1. what stage fright is
2. what causes it
3. how to make all your butterflies fly in formation

"Pray God our greatness may not fail,
Thro' craven fears of being great."
—*Alfred, Lord Tennyson*

SCARED STIFF

I have met people who became so frightened at the prospect of getting up before a group that they simply could not function. Yet, there are speakers who actually seem to thrive on stage fright. They perform better and enjoy it more when they are tense going into a big speaking engagement.

When Does It Go Away?

"How long does it take before you can speak without feeling any stage fright?" a beginning speaker asked me after I had been speaking professionally for about eight years.

"I'll let you know when it happens," I replied. The fact is it never completely disappears.

For example, I was scheduled to do a program at Edwards Air Force Base in California just one week after the 1986 Challenger shuttle disaster. NASA does a lot of its training at Edwards Air Force Base, and they also land the space shuttles there when the weather on the East Coast is unsuitable. The people I was doing the seminar for were very much involved with the shuttle program and with that tragic mission. Not sure how to act or what to say, I was very apprehensive and concerned about how receptive an audience I would find.

In a situation like that, simple reassurances do not help much. When I checked with the meeting planner before the program, his reaction was, "Well, we're all pros and, while it was a real tragedy, these tragedies have been occurring for many, many years. . . . These people have learned to live with that." But even as I stood to speak, I felt very anxious about the whole situation, which was extremely difficult for me to handle.

As it turned out, that audience was great. Certainly the people were heartbroken, but they knew they had to keep going on with the work their coworkers had died for. If anything, they were more committed than ever and more eager to learn. While it is a beautiful experience to remember, it was frightening to face.

What is stage fright? What causes it? What can you do about it? Let's look for some answers to those questions.

WHAT IS STAGE FRIGHT?

According to a study of 50,000 college students conducted recently by West Virginia University, the typical person is "deathly afraid" of public speaking. Of the students sampled, 70 percent experienced great anxiety before speaking to a large audience with 40 percent or more becoming afraid when faced with addressing as few as six to eight people.

"The formulation of a problem is far more essential than its solution," said Albert Einstein, who was one of the world's greatest thinkers and problem solvers. He went on to say that you cannot solve a problem until you understand clearly what that problem is.

Stage Fright's Real Name Is Stress

Stress is a master of disguise, and one of its masks is stage fright. Dr. Hans Selye, who was perhaps the world's foremost authority on stress, defined it as "the body's response to any demand placed on it, whether that demand is shocking grief or pleasant relief."[1]

Our muscles tense, our heart rate rises, our breathing becomes shallow and rapid, and our glands secrete adrenalin and other chemicals. It is our physical response to danger or excitement.

In other words, stress (alias stage fright) is not what happens to us, it is *our reaction* to what happens, or what we think might happen to us. We create our own stress. Although we don't always create the circumstances which give rise to pressure, we do create the stress itself.

Many people think of stage fright as something which other people or circumstances do to them. You have certainly heard someone say, "It makes me nervous!" or "You make me so mad...!" or "I just can't help being uptight!" Maybe you've said things like that to yourself and others.

The good news is that if we create stress for ourselves, we can control it.

Stage Fright Is Not All Bad

"To varying degrees, we thrive on stress," said Dr. Selye. "In fact, stress is the spice of life."[2]

Our stage fright often comes from choosing, from striving, from taking on big challenges, and even from the good things which happen to us. Take away those things and life becomes

---

[1] Hans Selye, M.D., quoted in *Success Unlimited Magazine*, September, 1980, p. 18, 19.
[2] Ibid.

bland, dull, and uninteresting. We lose our competitive edge, our intensity, and our drive.

Sometimes, it comes from the sheer excitement and enthusiasm we feel. Our body does not know the difference between excitement and terror, any more than it knows the difference between real and imagined danger. So, according to Dr. Selye, it reacts to excitement in precisely the same way it reacts to fear.

Some of the most outstanding speakers in the world say that the tension they feel drives them to excel at public speaking. "Any time I feel complacent or nonchalant about a speech, I get worried about my attitude," said one of America's most successful speakers.

So the key is not to eliminate all stress, but to learn how to control it and to make it work for you instead of against you.

Learn To Identify Stage Fright

Since stage fright often shows up in annoying symptoms, one of the first priorities is learning how to recognize those symptoms and what they do to you.

Here are some of the more common ways symptoms show up:

- *physical symptoms:* dry mouth, tense throat muscles, quaking voice, trembling or shortness of breath
- *cognitive symptoms:* loss of ability to concentrate, being forgetful or humorless
- *emotional symptoms:* being fearful, easily upset or agitated
- *behavioral symptoms:* drinking more alcohol, eating too much, eating more sweets, or acting irrationally

Stage fright shows up differently in all of us. For some, it may show up as knocking knees or trembling hands. Others may feel like the guy who said, "When I stand up to speak, my mind sits down." What's important is to identify the ways that stage fright affects you most often so you can deal with those specific symptoms.

WHAT CAUSES STAGE FRIGHT?

Earlier, I said that we cause our own stage fright. Of course we don't get up one morning and decide "I think I'll be uptight today." What we do is to hold onto certain attitudes and engage in certain actions which result in stage fright (alias stress).

Let's look at some of the ingredients we use to cook up our own pots of stewing or boiling stage fright. Later we'll explore some tested and proven methods of dealing with them. Often, just recognizing that we do certain things can help us to overcome them and the problems they create.

Stage Fright Ingredient 1:
Unrealistic Expectations Of Ourselves

Many of us hold ideals for ourselves which would even intimidate a superhero. We often expect ourselves to accomplish more in a short speech than any human could possibly get done in years.

Some of us seem to think we will fail utterly unless we deliver the greatest talk ever given, move that audience as no one has ever moved a group of people, and convince everyone present that we are the most brilliant human who ever lived. Thus, we set goals for ourselves we can never reach; then we react to the pressures we have created by becoming tense, anxious, and frightened.

By the time we rise to speak, our self-expectations are so high, and our composure so low, that we feel we must operate at a level far beyond our abilities. Unfortunately, the more we do this to ourselves, the more we feel like failures and the less we expect to succeed.

Stage Fright Ingredient 2:
Unrealistic Expectations Of Others

Just as we tend to expect too much from ourselves, we also tend to expect too much from others. We may look to others to make us happy, to provide for our emotional needs, and to build our self-esteem.

For example, we may expect others to appreciate the thorough job we have done of researching a speech, or expect others to say it was the greatest speech they have ever heard. We may even hope a speech will convince others that we are right and they are wrong. When the "others" don't come through as we think they should, we become angry, frustrated, and stressful. The problem is not with others; it is with our unrealistic expectations of them.

Stage Fright Ingredient 3:
Self-Fulfilling Prophecies Of Doom

Some of us create our own stage fright by predicting the worst outcomes from all our actions, circumstances or failures. We carry on a constant conversation with ourselves, saying "I can't!" or "This is really a tough speech!" or "I'm just not cut out to be a speaker!"

We may play subconscious mind games with ourselves. For example, if we stumbled through a reading assignment in the third grade and the whole class laughed at us, we may subconsciously tell ourselves, "It's going to happen all over again. . . . I just know it!"

Such self-defeating statements weaken our effectiveness, sometimes to such a degree that immobilizing panic sets in. When added to our unrealistic expectations, the combination can be a killer.

Stage Fright Ingredient 4:
Overreaction

You may be one of those people who sees every speech as the one to end all speeches. If so, you can bring a great deal of stage fright on yourself.

For example, a person who overreacts might imagine, "If I say that today, I'll be fired for sure!" or "I just know they're going to think I've flipped." Sometimes people will rehearse their excuses and explanations and predict they won't be received or believed.

Usually, overreaction is based on deep-seated fears and insecurities. Fears of failure, criticism, or rejection often show up most vividly when we have to stand before a group. Fortunately, most of our dire expectations never come to pass. Yet the fear we allow them to create for us can sometimes bring on even greater symptoms and problems.

Stage Fright Ingredient 5:
Worry And Anxiety

Stage fright is often caused by excessive worry and anxiety. "What happens if the p.a. system goes out?" or "What if they have already heard my stories?" or "What will I do if my throat gets dry?"

Worry is like a wart, useless and ugly; yet many of us do more than our share of it. It can become such a habit that we may worry about not having a pressing concern to worry about. "I must be overlooking something!" a worrier may exclaim.

To make it even worse, anxiety feeds on itself and grows stronger. The more we worry, the more we find to be anxious about. By the time we stand up to speak, we are convinced that nothing will go right.

Stage Fright Ingredient 6:
Unnecessary Time Pressures

Some of us seem to feel time will stand still and wait for us to do all we would like to do each day. We cram our days full of activities, promising others we will do time-consuming things and accepting even some of the most unrealistic requests and orders. As a result, our days become impossibly full and our nights so booked there is no time left to relax. Even when we do have free time, we are so concerned about the things we "should be doing" that relaxation eludes us.

Time moves on relentlessly. It never stops to ask if we have taken the time to prepare ourselves for an upcoming speech or presentation. When the appointed day arrives, it suddenly dawns upon us that we are not ready. What's more, we are exhausted from all our running and lack of rest, so we feel trapped and nervous about the outcome.

THE POINT IS...

The point of all this is that it is not circumstances nor others that create stage fright for us; it's something we do to ourselves. We do it by our unrealistic expectations of ourselves and others, making self-fulfilling prophecies of doom, overreacting, worrying, and creating unnecessary time pressures. We have mentioned only a few of the more common ways people create and intensify stage fright. You may have additional ingredients of your own.

HOW TO MAKE ALL YOUR BUTTERFLIES
FLY IN FORMATION

As a college football coach, I met many guys who looked like Mack trucks and were so tough they'd take on a whole team by themselves. But let one of those "monster-men" win an award and be called upon to say a few words for a group of fans, he would come apart at the seams.

No one is immune to stage fright. It afflicts men and women, chief executives and line workers, salespeople and engineers, amateur and professional speakers. The bottom line is that to make it as a high-impact person in almost any profession, you have to face up to it and continue to function.

"I accept the fact that I'm going to have butterflies in my

stomach every time I speak," said a seasoned professional speaker. "I only want to get them to fly in formation."

That's a clever way of paraphrasing General Omar Bradley's famous statement that "Bravery is the capacity to perform properly even when scared half to death."

Certainly there is an amount of courage involved in standing still while your knees are trying to do a break-dance. I especially admire those people who stand tall on the outside, even while they are drawn up into a little ball on the inside.

There is, however, a great deal you can do both to reduce and control the effects of stage fright. Let me offer some pointers I have learned from years of experience and from some of the best speakers I have ever met.

Control Pointer 1:
Keep It In Perspective

When you have made as many speeches as I have, you begin to recognize some comforting things about stage fright. First, you notice that it is almost never fatal. A good clue is that many speakers (like Dr. Peale) who have lived with stage fright throughout their careers are still going strong at seventy, eighty, and beyond.

Second, you begin to recognize that you are not alone in feeling it. Almost everywhere you go, someone wants to talk about it.

Third, you discover that you can function quite adequately, no matter how much pressure you feel.

Fourth, you sense that the stage fright you feel is not quite as keen as it was in the early days, or at least you don't let it matter as much to you.

Finally, you begin to suspect that Plato was right when he said, "Nothing in the affairs of men is worthy of great anxiety."

Eventually you learn to hold it all in proper perspective. After all, even though an audience could charge the podium and cover you with tar and feathers, they almost never do. They could throw things at you, but it's not likely. They could verbally cut you to shreds, but a far more common response is apathy.

With experience comes the kind of confidence that shows stage fright up for the toothless tiger it really is. After you learn to live with it, you sometimes even enjoy having it around to keep you on your toes.

Control Pointer 2:
Don't Make It Worse

We have seen at least six indirect ways we can make stage fright worse, but there are direct actions speakers often take to really turn up the heat on themselves—at the very time they need to cool things down. Here are three of the most common ways speakers can make it worse.

1.   What's the first thing most speakers do when they feel frightened? They apologize! They offer excuses for their lack of preparation, their lack of skill, or the circumstances. Apologizing is like holding up a huge sign that says, "I'm not expecting much so don't you expect much!"

Unfortunately, Benjamin Disraeli was right: "Apologies only account for that which they do not alter." Apologies and excuses do not change your shortcomings, they only call attention to them.

Let me give you my law of minimizing stage fright and maximizing effectiveness: "*Never* apologize or offer excuses to an audience!" Instead, get on with what you have to say and give it your best shot. You'll be miles ahead.

2.   Another common way speakers turn up the heat for themselves is by letting the audience see them squirm. They may even publicly admit to being scared. In effect, they announce how scared they are, how incompetent they feel, and in effect ask the audience not to take them seriously.

Ironically, if they would keep quiet about it, no one would ever notice their fear. So they add to their own problems.

You might get the sympathy of an audience by telling them you are scared, but you will not gain their respect and admiration. Most of all, you will not gain their favor, which is so vital to making a strong impact. Performing before an audience is a little like playing poker. If you don't show what you're holding, they'll take you a lot more seriously.

Never admit to being scared. Guard against the telltale signs of stage fright. Don't fidget with the lectern, the mike, or your papers. If your hands are trembling, keep them moving. Get on with what you came to do. Get involved with the audience and concentrate on what you have to say. You'll be surprised at how much it will relax you.

3.   Sometimes, speakers make their stage fright worse by taking themselves so seriously that they lose their sense of humor. While it is true that unless you take yourself seriously, no one else

will, it is equally true that if you take yourself too seriously, you'll lose your perspective.

I find it relaxing to myself and to my audiences to begin my speeches by cracking jokes about myself. Of course, I am very careful about how I do it. For example, I insist that I first be introduced properly, and I am careful not to put myself down. I tell stories about experiences that happened when I was much younger, things that happen to everybody, and things that are so ridiculous I know that no one will believe them.

When the audience sees that I am willing to laugh at myself, they feel free to laugh with me. And if I make a blooper, I laugh right along with the audience. Then I take advantage of it to regain control by telling them about another boner I once made. It's great for building rapport and also can be a lot of fun.

Whatever you do, don't make your stage fright worse by apologizing, offering excuses, letting the audience see you squirm, or by taking yourself too seriously.

Control Pointer 3:
Learn How To Relax Away Stress

Just as your body has built-in mechanisms to help you prepare for emergencies, it has mechanisms to help you relax.

In a book titled *The Relaxation Response,* Herbert Benson, M.D.[3] describes a simple but very effective way to relax. Simply take a few deep breaths and concentrate on relaxing your body. The secret is in the deep breathing, according to Dr. Benson. In research for Harvard Medical School, he and his team found that the body needs a signal to relax, just as it needs a signal to get tense.

The simplest way to relax is (1) get comfortable, (2) focus on a simple object or phrase, (3) concentrate on relaxing, and (4) take a few deep breaths. That will signal to your body that it is time to calm down.

Of course, you cannot very well stop in the middle of a speech and start deep-breathing exercises. But that is not usually when you need most to relax. It is when you first begin that stage fright takes its worst toll.

The best approach is to do it just before you are introduced to speak. If you practice enough, you can learn to do it so naturally that no one will never notice.

[3] Herbert Benson, *The Relaxation Response* (New York: Morrow, 1975).

Another helpful approach is to practice breathing more slowly and deeply in the normal course of life, and mentally associate the deeper breathing with relaxing. It is a great way to stay relaxed and to make deep breathing the most natural way for you to breathe. The more naturally you breathe, the less your audience will notice your breathing, and the more pleasant you will sound.

Practice taking deep breaths, often and in short deep-breathing exercises. But when you speak, try to take in only the amount of air that is comfortable for you.

Control Pointer 4:
Build Self-Confidence

"People who feel good about themselves produce good results,"[4] say Blanchard and Johnson in *The One-Minute Manager*. In other words, the more competent you feel and the more committed you are to what you are saying, the better you will do as a speaker.

The master key to feeling competent is the dynamic duo of preparation and practice. When you have prepared so completely that you know precisely what you are going to say and how you are going to say it, you feel confident that you can cope with whatever arises. And when you have practiced enough that you can give your speech forward or backwards, you can focus all your attention on building rapport with your audience.

Commitment simply means you believe that what you have to say is worth saying to the best of your ability. When what you have to say matters enough to you, you will find a way to say it with enthusiasm and impact.

Remember, your self-confidence will always be in direct proportion to how well you have prepared, how much you have practiced, and how committed you are to what you have to say.

Control Pointer 5:
Make Friends With The Audience

A businessman was to be given an award by an organization to which he belonged. When told that he would be asked to say a few words at the dinner, he was scared to death. He had never made a speech in his life.

---

[4] Kenneth Blanchard and Spencer Johnson, *The One Minute Manager* (New York: Berkley, 1981), p. 19. Copyright 1981 by Blanchard Family Partnership and Candle Communications Corporation. Published by permission of William Morrow & Co., New York.

The evening arrived and the businessman found himself seated on the platform next to the main speaker of the evening, a man with a national reputation for witty and entertaining after-dinner talks.

"I'm supposed to say a few words," confided the businessman, "and I can't think of anything to say. In fact, I'm terrified."

The guest speaker smiled sympathetically. "I know just how you feel," he said. "I've made hundreds of speeches, yet I'm probably just as scared as you are."

The businessman was surprised. "But *you* don't have to be afraid!"

"Neither do you," said the speaker. "Let me tell you a secret, then you'll never be troubled again. Everyone on earth is shy and self-conscious underneath. All of us are timid about meeting strangers, whether singly or in a group like this."

"That audience out there," continued the speaker, "is as scared as you are. Make *them* feel relaxed and comfortable with you, and you'll forget your own fears and you'll make a fine speech."

He did—it worked! It always does!

The more you can think of the audience as "we" and "us," and the less you think of them as "you" and "they," the less isolated and afraid you'll feel. In fact, I like to get among the people as quickly as I can. I find it helps to get them involved in what I am doing—to make the presentation something we are doing together.

So, make friends with your audience as soon as you can; it's a lot easier to relax among friends.

SO, WHAT HAVE WE SAID?

Stage fright is a normal part of public speaking, and some of it can actually help to keep you sharp. But too much of even a good thing can lessen your impact and make your life miserable.

Your best bet is to:

1. Understand what stage fright is and how it affects you. It is a form of stress, and it affects each of us differently.
2. Recognize that it comes from your reactions, and not from the audience or the circumstances. Since you create it, you can control it.
3. Follow a few simple pointers to keep it under control—no matter what happens.

ACTION STEPS

1. Make a list of the specific ways stage fright causes the most problems for you and come up with strategies (based on what you have read) to deal with each of them.

2. List ways you might be making stage fright worse for yourself and how you can use the pointers in this chapter to change those patterns.

3 HOW TO GET STARTED WITH A BANG

PURPOSE

The first two minutes of your speech are the most crucial. That is when the audience will decide either to sit up and listen or drift off into their own thoughts.

Together, we will explore:

1. what a good opening can do for you
2. how to come on strong from the start
3. how to make them want to hear more

> "A journey of a thousand miles begins with a single step."
> —*Old Chinese Proverb*

MAKE EVERY SPEECH AN EVENT

As public speakers, we are performers, just as much as professional stage actors, musicians, and singers. So, why is it that most people say "I went to *see* a rock concert (or popular singer)," while they say "I went to *hear* a speaker"?

One great reason is that professional performers have learned to make every performance an event, a happening which people experience. They put on a show that moves their audience. But, unfortunately, most public speakers merely "give a talk," or "make a few remarks." Their audiences could gain as much from reading their remarks or from hearing them talk on an audio cassette.

High-impact public speakers take their cues from the top professional performers; they make every speech an event—something for their audience to experience.

In this chapter, we explore how you can start every speech with a bang.

WHAT A GOOD OPENING CAN DO FOR YOU

A good opening does at least three things:

1. It creates a receptive climate for your speech by making the audience feel they can trust you, and that you have something important or entertaining to say to them. It sets the tone for the whole speech.
2. A good opening introduces speaker and audience to each other. It gives the audience insight as to where the speaker is coming from, and gives the speaker a chance to get a feeling for what it takes to get the desired response.
3. It introduces your speech. It lets people know what you will be talking about and why they should listen to you.

Thus, the most important part of the speech is that critical first two or three minutes, when the audience decides to either nod off until you finish or sit up and take notice of what you have to say.

It's Where You Grab 'Em

One of my favorite stories tells of an old mountain minister who sold a mule to his neighbor, but only after the neighbor had agreed to speak kindly and be gentle with the aging animal.

"Why, I won't have any problems being gentle with that

mule," replied the neighbor, explaining that the mule was known throughout the area as the best work animal around.

But a week later the neighbor was back with the complaint, "I can't get that mule to do anything!" even though he had spoken kindly and "treated him like I would a baby."

"Hummm!" said the old minister, and offered to correct the problem. Together, they went to where the mule stood hitched to a plow. The minister walked around in front of the mule, picked up a stick, and clobbered him right between the eyes.

The mule dropped to his knees, then slowly got up. Just as he stood, his former owner hit him again, "Bang!"

The neighbor protested, "I don't understand! I thought you said I should only speak kindly to him!"

"Yeah!" drawled the old man, "But first you've gotta get his attention!"

Of course, I do not want to even remotely suggest you do it that way, but I strongly suggest you open every talk with a big "bang" of your own. Let's look at some of the most powerful tools for getting people to sit up and take notice when you start to speak. Your impact as a speaker will skyrocket as you develop the skills for doing each of them.

COME ON STRONG FROM THE START

The major television networks often spend as much as $100,000 or more on the main title for a series of shows. The main title is that first ten or twenty seconds you see as the show comes on.

Now, why would those tight-fisted business people spend so much money on music and images that last only a few seconds? It's because they know it works. Their research has revealed that many people leave their television sets on for a few seconds, after watching a show, to see what's coming on next. The producers know they have only ten—at most twenty—seconds to lure those viewers into watching another show. Since the size of their audiences determines how much money they can make, they consider it a good investment to grab all the viewers they can.

High-impact public speakers operate on the same principles. They know they have only a minute or two to gain the attention of their audiences. So they have developed some very effective opening techniques to help them do just that.

Opening Technique 1: Make Sure You Are Introduced Correctly

Actually, impact begins with a strong introduction of the speaker. It is vital that you have a formal introduction that is read with enthusiasm by a third party. Mine is very carefully worded and is designed to make me sound like the kind of person an audience wants to hear.

Most meeting planners will ask you for information that can be used in introducing you. Take that as your cue to put together a top-notch introduction—one that is honest and short, but one that really sells you to that audience.

Many amateur speakers shy away from asking for a good introduction because they feel it is akin to bragging. What we are talking about is not "tootin' your own horn," but making it clear to the audience that you are someone who will have something worthwhile to say to them.

Having a succinct but complete prepared introduction is one of the best ways to avoid having someone drone on and on with syrupy comments about you that are meaningless. Audiences would rather hear an adequate introduction than listen to vague remarks from a person who loves to talk.

Opening Technique 2: Get Properly Grounded

One of the things I try to avoid is becoming ungrounded. This simply means you're not in touch with your audience. I'm sure you have been in audiences where a speaker was droning on about something nobody cared about or telling meaningless stories. Such speakers are so completely out of touch with their audiences that people are not listening: they are gazing off into space. It just isn't working.

The first thing you can do to become grounded is to learn how to read your audience properly and stay in touch with them at all times. One basic technique is to find out as much as you can about an audience and the circumstances surrounding your scheduled speech as far in advance as possible.

One of the toughest speeches I ever did was for a Swiss-owned company. As you might imagine, I had to cope with cultural differences. There were Americans, Canadians, Germans, Italians, Dutch, and Swiss people in that diverse audience.

After studying the situation, I knew I would have to be careful to speak more slowly than I normally do. Another adjustment I would have to make was to remember that there are definite limits on what you can do with humor. Since humor is so much a part of my style, I occasionally tried slipping in a little, but I had to be very careful not to lose parts of my audience. Usually, it went over very well, but I noticed that the Americans would howl, while some of the Europeans would laugh a little and some were totally lost.

Through research, I also discovered that the European style of presentation is much more formal than the American style, so I knew I would have to keep jumping between the formal and the informal. In sum, before I ever got to the platform, I knew I had to speak slowly, could not use much humor, and had to make sure the Europeans understood while not boring the Americans.

It was a tough assignment, but I was grateful that I had studied my audience so thoroughly in advance.

Second, size up the audience while you are waiting to be introduced. Many speakers sit bored while they are waiting to go on stage. Not me! I have found it helps to use every minute of that valuable time to read that audience and make any needed last-minute adjustments. Some of those lessons came the hard way.

A large aircraft manufacturing company once invited me to do a seminar for its supervisors. But the meeting planner said that what he wanted to do was to place my seminar in the middle of the week, when the people had been through a succession of routine things. He wanted me to do a highly energized motivational program geared toward personal productivity and time management.

I did my best. Unfortunately, what had happened was that the meeting planner had misread the group. There was not an executive in that audience who supervised less than 4,000 to 5,000 people. When my program was done, I got feedback like "amateurish," "high school," or "rah, rah cheerleader." That style worked very well the next day with a different group, but it bombed with those executives.

Although the meeting planner had certainly misread the group, more important, I as a speaker had misread the group. Looking back, I think I should have sized that audience up and said, "Look, my reading of this group is different from that of the meeting planner."

Third, stay sensitive to your audience from the first moment until you close the talk. If somebody is drifting away, work toward that person's attention; try to find something that turns that person on. Usually, if something you do turns the most distant person on, it will be dynamite for those who are tracking you.

Opening Technique 3: Master Nonverbals

High-impact speakers know they have to sell themselves before they can sell their ideas. One of the greatest obstacles to overcome in speaking is the tension your audience feels. Psychologists tell us that one of the great obstacles you must overcome in speaking is the "territorial imperative" phenomenon. At the beginning of your speech, the audience thinks of you as an outsider—an invader, if you please—and they size you up very carefully in the first few minutes. In that crucial minute or two, you will create either tension or trust; you will either gain a favorable hearing, or you will close the door.

So the real high-impact speakers work from the outset to help people relax and trust them. They know that the mind is most open when it is relaxed.

What you may not realize is that about 90 percent of what makes people relax and trust you is nonverbal. It has to do with the way you look and what you do. In fact, the visual impact you create goes much farther in building trust than does anything you say.

If you question that, think about the ways you react differently, according to the ways people look and act. For example, if a sharply dressed person walks briskly into your office and announces he or she would like to see your boss, you probably sit up and take notice. But if a ragged and dirty street bum saunters in off the street and starts snooping around, you probably react quite differently. More than anything else, you are reacting to the way the person looks and acts. You quickly decide that the one person is important (because he or she looks important), but that the other person has nothing worthwhile to say or do in your office. That same principle is at work when you stand before an audience.

As a rule, I always try to dress slightly better than the best dressed people in my audience. I take special pains to look my best in every detail.

Next, I try to exude confidence and enthusiasm as I walk to the speaker's stand. I want those people to know that I am glad to be there, that I want to be their friend, and that I am going to do all I can to make our time together enjoyable and pleasant. I also want them to feel that I know exactly why I am there, and that I can do precisely what I came to do.

Once I am standing in front of the group, the first thing I do is give the audience a great big smile. It's my way of saying, "Relax, I won't hurt you!"

The way you look and what you do—more than anything you say—determines how much your audience relaxes and trusts you. I urge you to read some of the many excellent books on nonverbal communication.

Opening Technique 4: Crash Through The Ice Barrier

One of the hazards of public speaking is that most audiences are subjected to reports, dull speakers, introductions, and announcements—all before you speak. As a result, the term "ice barrier" is an apt description of what you will confront when you stand before the group.

The most effective technique for breaking through the ice barrier is to use humor. What I do after a strong introduction that makes me look good is start cracking one-liners and telling stories about myself. These are carefully thought out and have a clear purpose. I want to come across to that audience as a "regular guy," someone they can relate to and connect with. I want to put them at ease and let them know that I want the same things they want and struggle with the same things they do.

Since I spent many years as a football coach, I use a lot of stories about football. These are not hackneyed stories that everybody has heard; they are jokes that I know will work because I have used them hundreds of times. Basically it is a mechanical process. I use these stories on such a regular and consistent basis that I have confidence in them. Even more important, I am so familiar with them I can do them with little or no thought. That way, I can direct my attention to reading how the audience is responding to them.

Other excellent speakers use techniques such as making a powerful and controversial opening statement, or offering a fantastic benefit, or calling someone up from the audience and getting him or her to do something with them.

It is important that you find a technique that works well with your style and personality. Choose those that go over big with the audiences you most frequently perform for, and work on them until you can do them with finesse and power.

Nothing you can do will ever give you more impact than developing a strong technique for crashing through the ice barrier and connecting with your audience.

Opening Technique 5: Take Control Early And Make It Stick

Everything changes when you stand up to speak to an audience. You may know every person in that audience, you may have talked many times with each of them, and you may be considered by them as "just one of the boys or girls." But when you stand before the group, it's all different. In our last chapter, we saw how that very factor scares some speakers half to death. But high-impact speakers know that being the center of attention is what speaking is all about, and that most audiences actually want it that way.

There is, however, a great deal of difference in being granted the vaunted position of center of attention and earning the respect that goes with that position. People who come to hear you expect you to take control early and make it stick. For example, studies show that most audiences become irritated by hecklers. They may laugh at the first two or three jibes from within the audience, but they will actually turn on the speaker if he or she does nothing to stop the hecklers.

To take control early and keep it means that you make it clear that you will determine the topic to be discussed, the tempo of the discussion, and the mood of the session. But it is a control that must be earned, not one that comes automatically. Obviously, you do not gain respect by simply telling an audience you are in charge. A far better approach is to set a pace that everyone present will want to follow.

Taking charge means convincing the audience that you are capable of handling the trust they have shown by inviting you. Again, we are talking about the way you look, the self-confidence you exude, and the way you use nonverbal messages.

We are also talking about the way you handle the topic you want to discuss. For example, speakers who open with statements like "I'm certainly no expert on this subject..." or "Most of you probably know much more about this subject than I do," are abdicating control—not gaining control. If you are not an expert, why speak in the first place? If everyone present knows more than you do, why not sit down and let them talk?

High-impact speakers never address an audience unless they have something worthwhile to say to them, and they assume control so they can say it. Certainly, I do not know more about the practice of medicine than a group of doctors at a seminar, so I will not talk about practicing medicine. But since I do know more than most of them about time management, I'll come on like gangbusters about time management.

Taking charge means that you make it clear you have something important to say about what you came to speak on. You can do that by the illustrations and stories you use in the opening, the statistics and authorities you quote, and the power of the statements you make about the subject.

Taking charge also means you must not let anybody in the audience repeatedly disrupt what you are trying to do. I make it a practice to follow a three-step formula for dealing with disrupters.

1. I first try to put them down in a gentle way.
2. If that doesn't work, I lower the boom on them.
3. If they persist in being disruptive, I will ask the audience "Do you want to hear this guy, or me?" They always say they want to hear me, so I give the heckler the choice of either calming down or being removed.

One reason this approach works so well for me is my football coaching background, and the fact that I look like a man who can take care of himself.

Whatever tactics you use, never let a disrupter destroy your position at the head of that group. If you do, you are dead.

In short, what you do is take charge early and make it stick by earning the respect of your audience, by convincing them you can handle the topic, and by dealing forcefully with hecklers.

Opening Technique 6: Get The Audience Involved

High-impact speakers always seek to involve their audiences from the very beginning. They know that an involved audience is an interested audience.

I often speak to real estate salespeople in various groups throughout the country, and they have taught me a lot about getting people involved. Sharp real estate salespeople tell me they look for every way possible to enable a prospect to "experience ownership."

For example, before a prospect will take actual ownership, he or she must experience psychological ownership. They say you can tell the moment it happens by the language the prospect uses. As long as they are talking in terms of *"You would have to* fix the roof," the house stills belongs to the original owner. But the moment they start saying things like *"I will* have to get rid of that awful green paint," they have taken psychological ownership.

Not only can you tell when it happens, you can make it happen. The way you do it is to look for every conceivable way for the members of your audience to feel that what you have to say matters greatly to them personally.

To get your audience involved, identify with them verbally in every possible way. The key to all effective communication is *identification*. "That which is most personal is most interesting," said philosopher and psychologist William James.

Get physically involved with the audience. I like to have a portable mike with a long cord so I can actually move out into the audience, which gives me the best of both worlds. Since I am the only one standing, I still have their attention. And, since I am moving out among them, I can more quickly overcome the "we/they" attitude. In a later chapter, we will discuss what to do while you rove through the audience, but for now let me say that the earlier you can get physically involved with them, the more quickly you can get them involved.

Many very successful speakers open by having the audience do something. They may have the audience stand briefly, or lead them in a round of applause for the meeting planners, or use one of a number of other tactics. Their reason for having the audience do something is that it subconsciously says, "Hey, I'm in charge here!" It really works.

Another very effective technique for getting the audience involved is to use visual or mental exercises. For example, you might open by showing a group of common objects (a paper clip, a rubber band, a watch) on an overhead projector for about fifteen seconds, then turn the projector off and ask them to write down all the things they can remember. Later, you read a list of the objects and ask each person to check his or her powers of observation. This is a great way to launch a speech on overlooking the obvious.

There are many such exercises available in books and magazines, but with a little creativity you can invent your own. To make them work, they need to be simple and fun, they must make a strong but obvious point, and they must be grounded in what you plan to speak about.

What it all means is that the more you involve your audience, the quicker and more completely you can connect with them.

Opening Technique 7: Keep Working At It Until You Connect

Remember that effective public speaking begins the moment you have the full attention of your audience, and not one second sooner.

That means if you don't get their attention on the first try, keep trying until you do. Believe me, that is not always easy to do. For example, you may run into circumstances beyond your control which make it hard for an audience to hear anything you have to say.

I recently did a speech for a large wholesale sporting goods group. I was hired to speak to their convention at a luncheon. As it happened, they were going through a tremendous business downturn. They were experiencing much internal conflict within the organization; their industry was in turmoil, they were not making much money, and they felt as if they were being cut out by the manufacturers.

To make it even worse, I was standing in for another speaker who was primarily a humorist, so I felt they wanted something that was funny. For about five minutes, I died as I used my absolute best material—material that I know will always work—and I got no laughs. That material had been tested and proven literally hundreds of times. I have learned that if you have material that you know always works, and that material does not work, it's not the material—it's the group.

Well, I have been through that sort of thing before, so I shifted gears, and went into some hard-core business material. However, they did not respond to that either. When I saw that was not getting through, I shifted into some inspirational material and finally got a reasonable response.

Interestingly, I got a letter from the meeting planner saying I was the best speaker they ever had. He explained that the audience just happened to be a low-key group. But I am convinced the reason that speech worked was that I kept shifting gears until I found a way to connect. You may have to change directions three or four times in order to salvage a program, but that is better than going ahead when you know you do not have full attention.

SO, WHAT HAVE WE SAID?

High-impact speakers work hard to make each of their speeches a real event, a happening which the audience can experience. In order to do that, they always come on strong from the beginning.

That means they:

—make sure they get introduced properly
—become grounded by reading their audience
—master the nonverbal messages they send
—find ways to crash through the ice barrier

—take charge early and make it stick
—get the audience involved with them

Most of all, they stay with it until they have connected with their audience.

If you practice these simple opening techniques, you will be amazed at how much more impact your speaking will have.

ACTION STEPS

1. Try to remember a time when you found it particularly hard to connect with an audience. As you review the seven opening techniques we have discussed, think about how you could have solved the problem with one or more of them.

2. Think about a speech you experienced and make a list of things the speaker did to make it an event you would always remember. See if you can uncover techniques you can use.

GIVE 'EM A SHOW THEY'LL NEVER FORGET

PURPOSE

Gaining favor as a high-impact speaker includes developing a good platform personality and manner. In this chapter, we seek to discover how you can give 'em a show they'll never forget, each time you speak.

Together, we will explore:

1. how to give 'em all you are
2. how to perform with power

> "Mend your speech a little, lest you alter your fortunes."
> —*William Shakespeare*

IN SEARCH OF HIGH IMPACT

Actor Richard Burton once performed the famous closing speech of King Arthur from Camelot on television's ever-popular *Tonight Show*.

If you saw the elaborate Broadway production of that show or its later movie version, you know that the setting of the speech depicted the legendary King Arthur of the mythical kingdom of Camelot just before he went into the final battle. In that battle, the king would be killed and all traces of his "perfect" kingdom would be forever destroyed.

The audience for the speech was one young boy who had offered to go with the king and fight to the death for the beloved kingdom.

"No, my boy," the king started, "You go back and tell all who will listen . . . that once there was a place called Camelot." He then went on to describe for the boy how "The rain may never fall 'til after sunset; by eight the morning fog must disappear; and there's a legal limit to the snow here, in Camelot."

As Richard Burton began with those opening lines, a hush fell over the usually raucous *Tonight Show* audience. His rendition of the piece was so dramatic that many in the audience were actually in tears before he finished. As the performance drew to a close, the audience sat in stunned silence for a moment, then broke into uproarious applause.

Host Johnny Carson was clearly deeply moved and noted that the speech was one of the all-time classics of the theater. "But, I'll tell you something," he then exclaimed, "Richard Burton could read pages from a telephone directory and keep people on the edge of their seats!"

By Way Of Contrast

Contrast that story with the one I heard about a young minister who was invited by the pastor of his own home church to give his first sermon after graduating from the seminary. Even though it's tough to speak with impact to an audience of people who know you very well, the young man decided to give it his best shot.

The great day came and he delivered the sermon he had spent weeks preparing. As the members of the congregation filed past him on their way out, they told him how nice he looked in his new robe, how obvious it was that he was a "gifted" preacher, and how they wished him well in his new work.

Finally, the young fellow stood face to face with his spunky aging grandmother, who was noted for always "tellin' it like it is."

"Well, how did I do, Granny?" he asked hopefully.

"Sonny," the old lady replied, "I only saw three things wrong!"

"That's not bad for my first sermon, Granny," the novice said. Then he asked the fatal question: "What were the three things I did wrong?"

"First, you read it! Second, you didn't read it well! And third, it wasn't worth reading, anyhow!" came the verdict.

Somehow, as I heard that story, it reminded me of a game called baseball. You know, "three strikes and you're out!"

What's The Difference?

Think for a moment about the two performances I have described and ask yourself the question, "What made the difference?" Better yet, think about the greatest speech you ever heard and ask yourself, "What made it so great?"

Certainly, the content of the speech must have been important to you at the time. If you are like most people, you probably cannot remember most of what the speaker said. But, even if you can, it's a safe bet you would not have been as impressed by merely reading the same information. That suggests there was something about the speaker's appearance, personality, or performance that grabbed your attention and made a lasting impact upon you. Chances are it was a combination of all three of those factors.

What we're really talking about is the elusive quality of stage presence, the ability to stand before a group and command the favor, respect, and rapt attention of every person present—a powerful platform manner. And it is an important element of what I call impact.

Either You Have It, Or You Don't?

There is little question that some speakers have a strong stage presence, while others simply do not. To get an idea of how pronounced it is, all you need to do is recall all the speeches you have seen and heard during the last year, and ask yourself which speakers you would like to hear again.

The big question is "Where does it come from?" Are speakers either born with it or without it? Does it come from stage techniques and mannerisms? If so, can it be cultivated?

It certainly seems that some people are born with an abundance of stage presence, owing perhaps to several factors. It may come from being born into a family which has a reputation for impact, such as the Kennedys. Or it may begin with a striking inner sense of the interests and concerns of masses of people. Abe Lincoln, for example, may have been born at the right place, at the right time. Sometimes, it seems to be a natural mystique or personal quality that causes people to sit up and take notice, such as with Sophia Loren.

Yet dozens of powerful stage and screen performers and speakers have become legendary without any of those "inborn" characteristics. Dr. Robert Schuller, President Ronald Reagan, and the late Peter Sellers are three who readily come to mind. None of the three would have been picked out of a crowd when they were young and singled out as destined for greatness. Yet each of them continuously made a profound impact on the audiences they sought to appeal to.

It seems very clear that whether you have stage presence or not, you can acquire it. For example, Demosthenes has often been called the greatest orator of ancient Greece, even though he had to compete with perhaps the finest orators of history. Yet Demosthenes was literally hooted off the stage halfway through his first attempt at addressing the city fathers of Athens. It was only after years of study, practice, and self-development that the young orator could hold an audience in the palm of his hand for hours.

What it all means is that stage presence is both a science and an art. It is a science because it has certain basic principles that underlie its operation; there are specific techniques which can produce definite and measurable results. Because it is also an art, there is no limit as to how good you can become at using high-impact stage techniques except, of course, how much of yourself you are willing to invest.

In the remainder of this chapter, we focus on those tested and proven platform techniques which can give you a strong stage presence. These stage presence "secrets" have worked very well for many of the greatest speakers in the world, but how well they work for you will be determined by how well you learn them and how much you practice using them.

HOW TO GIVE 'EM ALL YOU ARE

There are two things you very quickly notice about the best performers. First, they are good at consistency. They find what works best for them, practice it until they can do it very well, then stick to doing it until it becomes their own unique style.

For example, any time you see Dr. Norman Vincent Peale, you can count on hearing one or two very strong points, illustrated by countless stories. Don Rickles will always be cutting people to shreds, Joan Rivers will always be using sarcasm, and Perry Como will always be so relaxed he will look half asleep.

Second, they are consistently good. They're not dynamite one day and a dud the next. If you see them a dozen times, you see the same quality performance every time. Perhaps this is because they give every performance all they've got. They figure that if a group of people commit themselves to listen and watch, the least they can do is give them a show they'll never forget.

Here are some secrets they know which help them be consistently good by being good at consistency.

Stage Presence Secret 1: Go As A Total Person

People like winners. After many years of coaching and playing sports, I have concluded that real champions are always in great demand.

For example, Joe DiMaggio has been out of baseball for decades, yet his name still works magic and his face is one of the most recognized in America. Even people who care nothing about baseball call him a champ.

Whether it is public speaking, sports, or any other arena, real champions all have one characteristic separating them from the "also rans"—they give themselves totally to whatever they are doing. In other words, they don't just show up for the game; they play to win.

Of course, champion public speakers often make their performances look so easy that many people never suspect how much effort they put into it. Much of their stage presence comes from a deep desire to be their very best every time they perform.

Thus, when they go to speak, they go as a total person—body, mind, and spirit. You can see the desire in their eyes, feel the intensity in their mannerisms, and sense the full impact of their personality.

There is a lot more to you than you may have yet discovered. As you seek to bring the full impact of your total personhood to every speech you give, people will sense they are experiencing a high powered message and will listen intently to what you have to say.

Stage Presence Secret 2: Get Real; Gain Impact

In the early days of their development, public address systems were evaluated by how much they amplified the voice of the speaker, not by how accurately they reproduced his or her voice. As a result, speakers often sounded as if they were talking from inside a barrel and screaming at the top of their lungs.

Technology has now changed all that. Today, people who shop for p.a. systems look for the one that will most perfectly amplify every nuance of the speaker's voice and manner.

In a sense, this is what distinguishes public speaking from private conversation. Conversationalists seek to give individuals glimpses into their personhood; they want to make you feel what they feel. High-impact public speakers seek to reveal themselves to many people at once.

Call it sincerity or whatever you choose, people want to meet the real you when they hear you speak. If you want to have a powerful stage presence, get real! You may not have as powerful a personality as you would like to have, but your own personality is always the most powerful one available to you and to your audience while you are speaking. Think of speaking as nothing more than amplifying yourself to a whole roomful of individuals at a time.

Stage Presence Secret 3: Let Them Experience You

One thing that gives a speaker like Dr. Robert Schuller so much stage presence is that each person in an audience feels he is talking directly to them. He can speak to an audience of millions, one person at a time.

You get the feeling with such people that they are talking about people you know, that they are speaking to issues that are vital to you, and that they really care about what is on your mind. Thus, speakers with effective stage presence can make every person in an entire audience feel what they want them to feel, and care about what they want them to care about.

There are some definite techniques they use to achieve that kind of connection with their audiences, which leads us to our next major aspect in giving people a show they will never forget. People with powerful stage presence know they have to do more than just show up—they have to perform with power. Let's look at some of the tools they use to achieve consistently powerful performances.

PERFORM WITH POWER

The Reverend Billy Sunday was a fiery evangelist who, before the era of microphones, often moved audiences of 10,000 or more people to make deep commitments in response to his messages with only his voice and gestures. Obviously, here was a man who knew how to perform with power.

One of the most widely circulated stories about the celebrated evangelist is that he often wrote notes about his platform techniques in the margins of his sermon outlines. A biographer who was looking through his outlines after the famous minister's death found the frequent notation: "Shout loud! This is a weak point!"

Whether or not the story is true, you need only to look at his results to see that Billy Sunday must have made very strong points somewhere down the line, and that he also knew how to perform with power before an audience.

Let's examine some of the techniques that can give you more impact in your own speaking.

Performance Power Tool 1: Use Vocal Power

Although your voice may not be your only tool (or even your most effective one) for communicating your ideas, it is a vital one for speaking with power and impact.

"But I don't have a good speaking voice," you protest.

What I'm talking about is not possessing the tonal quality of an opera singer, but using what you have to maximum advantage. For example, I often refer to Dr. Norman Vincent Peale as one of the truly great speakers of our era. Yet, if you have ever had the high privilege of hearing him, you know that his voice could not be accurately described as tops in tonal quality. Like all great speakers, he has simply learned to use what he has; and he can make you want to hear more of anything he has to say.

I suggest that you cultivate as pleasant and forceful a speaking voice as you possibly can. Consider these elements of a pleasant and forceful voice:

1. *Clear diction.* That means saying words clearly and distinctly so people can understand every syllable. You can do this by minimizing your accent, especially if you speak in various areas of the country. Few things can create stronger barriers between you and your audience, or make you harder to understand, than a

strong but unfamiliar accent. The less pronounced it is, the easier it is for people of any region to understand and accept you.

The obvious exception is the performer whose accent is an asset in his or her act. For example, Jerry Clower's folksy stories from Yazoo City, Mississippi would not have nearly as much impact without his strong southern drawl.

2. *Good grammar.* The more you understand the English language and use it correctly, the more intelligent you will appear to be, and the more people will listen to what you have to say. Unless your goal is to appear as an ignorant country bumpkin, you can lend a great deal of credence to your speech if you use precise words and correct sentence structure. That means you not only have to study grammar and syntax, you need to work hard at breaking bad speaking habits.

Get rid of all slang words (like "ain't"), all jargon that may be unfamiliar to your audience, and all fad expressions which may date you. Avoid obvious errors such as double negatives, using nouns and verbs that do not match in gender or tense, and misplaced modifiers.

Simply stated, you have enough barriers to climb over without creating another one by misuse of grammar.

3. *Pleasant tone.* Your goal is to communicate, not to impress everybody with how pretty your voice is. On the other hand, the more pleasant your voice is, the easier you are to listen to for long periods. A good rule of thumb is that if people notice your voice, it is becoming a liability instead of an asset. Cultivate a pleasant tone that projects both your personality and message.

4. *Controlled volume.* If you have ever sat through a speech in which you could scarcely hear what was being said, or where the speaker droned on and on monotonously, you know how unpleasant it can be. It matters little what perfectly charming things you have to say unless people can hear you say them.

Even more important, varying your volume levels can do a great deal to help you add emphasis, entertain, and control the crowd. For example, I frequently go from very loud to very soft based upon the issue, the topic, the mood I am trying to create, and other factors. Even when I speak at a near whisper, I make sure every person in the room can hear me.

If you want to get a feeling for how it can work, listen to a great symphony on a fine stereo. Watch the volume meters to see how they jump from near distortion levels to registering almost no volume.

Performance Power Tool 2: Use Pacing For Interest And Impact

Pacing is critical because it is the way you make your audience move with you. If you can learn how to use variations in the speed at which you say things, you can keep an audience on the edge of their seats.

Here are some useful pointers on using pacing techniques:

1. *Use rhythm patterns to advantage.* All of us are geared to rhythm patterns, whether we realize it or not, but it affects each of us differently. The steady dripping of a faucet can drive some people right up a wall while it doesn't seem to bother others. Some people love the rhythm of rock n' roll music; others hate it.

But one thing that eventually gets to everybody is steady droning. That's why radio stations seldom play songs that last more than three minutes. Even if people love the songs, they get tired of hearing the same rhythm patterns and may switch stations. Vary the pace often, always keeping in mind the rhythm you are creating.

2. *Use pauses for impact.* You can use planned pauses not only to break monotony, but to create powerful impact.

Winston Churchill, for example, was a master at pausing for emphasis, but it was only after his death that the world learned those pauses were planned. "I always—well, most of the time—know exactly what I'm going to say, but I make believe, by hesitating a little, that a word or phrase has just come to me," he once told a friend. "I think the effect is improved." A well-placed pause might do wonders for your delivery.

3. *Vary your speed to stay up with your audience.* Studies show that most people can process about 750 words a minute. Since many people speak about 150 words per minute, the audience will often begin to wander into their own thoughts and get lost when there is a monotonous pace.

You can combat this problem by varying the pace. Slow down for emphasis, then speed up to force them to catch up with you. Occasionally, stop abruptly in the middle of a sentence, and jolt them into tracking with you.

Another excellent technique for pacing is to gear your speed to the content or to the mood you are trying to create. For example, if you are telling a story, fly through it to force them to stay with you to keep up with the action. But, when you are making a vital point, slow down dramatically.

Performance Power Tool 3: Use Humor To Keep Them With You

Critics of television have long called it everything from "a vast wasteland" to "the boob tube" because of its lack of intellectual content and formatting. Yet surveys show that more than 98 percent of the homes in America have television sets, which is more than have indoor plumbing.

The primary reason television is so popular and masses of people watch it, despite its dearth of intellectual appeal, is that people want to be entertained!

Likewise, the public speakers who are in great demand are those who understand that information had better also be entertaining or nobody will pay any attention to it. And the most frequent form of entertainment speakers use is humor.

Unfortunately, most speakers do not know much about using humor effectively. The following guidelines might prove helpful to you:

1. *Stay clear of shady material.* Don't use anything vulgar or off-color. Watch out for such poor taste remarks as ethnic slurs, sex biases, religious insults, and social or political controversies. With a little creativity, you will be amazed at how funny you can be without ever offending anyone.

2. *Identification is the key to impact.* Use things that people understand and care about. For example, I recently did a program for Europeans and, obviously, I did not use American football humor.

One of the most frequently overlooked factors about humor is that people look to it as an escape from their pains and fears. That's why comedian Jerry Lewis has been so popular for so many decades. He builds his humor around pathetic characters and painful situations that people can imagine themselves in, and audiences everywhere open up to him. I think he expressed it very well when he said, "Funny had better be sad somewhere."

The more people can identify with your jokes, the funnier they will think the jokes are.

3. *Make it move.* I try to use mostly one-line humor. Long, involved jokes that everyone has heard are seldom productive because people can become bored or lost in long, detailed jokes. Or, if someone tells you a joke and you use it in a speech, many people in your audience will have heard it because it is one of the jokes making the rounds.

Most important, long jokes can be hazardous to your impact. For example, if you invest three or four minutes in a story and then nobody laughs, you've wasted a lot of time. Do that two or three times in a half-hour talk, and you're losing your most precious moments. Besides, it can make you look like a real dummy.

4. *Relate all humor to what you are saying.* I have heard many speakers crack one joke after another, without ever coming close to the theme of their speech. Then they suddenly glance at their watch and say, "Well, we'd better move right along!"

Not only a waste of valuable time, this is also a waste of one of your most valuable resources for getting your points across. Nothing can drive home a vital point more forcefully than a good joke or one-liner which clarifies and emphasizes it.

Let me urge you to use a lot of humor and invest time in learning how to use it to good advantage. It is much more productive to spend time reading good books about why people laugh and how to make them laugh than it is to spend all your time looking for new jokes.

Performance Power Tool 4: Get Your Whole Body Into The Act

Earlier, we saw that about 90 percent of people's evaluation of whether or not to trust you and listen to what you have to say is nonverbal in nature and based more on what people see and perceive about you than on what you say.

But did you also know that about 75 percent of all communication is nonverbal? People watch you to see how you speak and what you are doing more than they actually listen to the words you use. If you smile, they relax and smile; if you scowl, they become tense and defensive. Likewise, if you stand rigidly behind the lectern and scarcely move, they become rigid both physically and mentally.

The larger the group, the more important nonverbal signals become. For example, if you are speaking in front of several thousand people, your gestures need to be broader and more pronounced. You also need to make your gestures slower, and hold them much longer than you would in conversation. It will also help to make your facial expressions more pronounced, almost exaggerated.

For example, if you watch Dr. Robert Schuller's *Hour of Power* television show, you'll notice how he uses grandiose gestures and long pauses while addressing the huge crowd in the Crystal Cathedral. Then, when he speaks to the television audience, he will pull everything in and put much more emphasis on his facial expressions. With his broad, sustained gestures, he is sending nonverbal messages to the large crowd, but his tight, limited gestures and facial expressions give you the feeling that he's talking directly to you.

It must work, because more than ten million viewers watch him every week.

Remember, your goal is to give your audience a *show* they'll never forget.

Performance Power Tool 5: Lay Ground Rules For Audience Control

Certain ground rules need to be clarified up front. That way, the audience knows that you are in charge and what to expect, and you save yourself a lot of hassles later on.

For example, are you going to allow time after your speech for questions, or are you going to take them throughout the program? The ground rules have to be set. If your topic is complex or controversial, or your audience is large, it might be good to ask everyone to hold all questions until the end. If you need more interplay with the audience, ask them to stop you along the way, and remind them periodically that you are open for their questions.

Also, make it clear up front that you will finish before the appointed time—then do it. If you get the reputation for respecting their time, they will give you respect in other ways.

Performance Power Tool 6: Use Visual Power

When we think of visual power, the image that most readily may come to mind is a projector and screen showing detailed shots or graphics. While this can be very helpful, visual power is not limited to slides, flip charts, and posters. If you are alert, you can often find something in the setting of the speech to get your points across with more impact.

One of the classic stories about using visual power is about the real estate salesman's use of a flowering cherry tree. The salesman took his clients to the backyard of a house he was trying to sell, and the woman shouted, "Oh! Look at that gorgeous cherry tree with all those blossoms all over it!"

"Do you like cherry trees?" the sharp salesman asked.

"I've always wanted a house with one in the yard." she gushed.

"Let's look inside." her husband said brusquely.

So they went inside. The man immediately started picking over things.

"The kitchen's mighty small," he grumbled.

"Yes, but look at the view of that blossoming cherry tree from this window."

When the man complained that the patio door needed repair, the salesman responded, "You can really see that cherry tree from here."

Upstairs, the guy commented about how poorly arranged the bedroom was, but the salesman led the woman to the window and pointed out the magnificent view of the cherry tree.

Eventually, he sold the blossoming cherry tree—and threw in the house as a bonus. Now, that's what I call using visual power!

What I'm trying to say is simply this: the more completely people in your audiences can connect what you say with what they are experiencing at the moment you are saying it, the greater will be its impact.

SO, WHAT HAVE WE SAID?

"I've always thought that the greatest symbol of common sense is building a bridge," said Franklin D. Roosevelt.

That's what stage presence is all about. It's that combination of personal attributes and carefully planned techniques that enables you to build a bridge across the gap that stands between you and your audience.

Giving people a show they'll never forget involves using power performance tools like:

1. carefully developed and skillfully used vocal power
2. pacing for maximum impact
3. well-conceived and relevant humor
4. getting your whole body into the act
5. laying out ground rules and following them
6. creativity in using visual power

As you take these tools as seriously as a scientist, and cultivate them with the sensitivity of an artist, you will be able to generate a great deal of power with any audience you address.

ACTION STEPS

1. List the three most outstanding performances you have ever seen and reflect on what the performer did to capture your attention.

2. Set up a plan to incorporate the ideas you found most attractive in this chapter into your own public speaking.

5 HOW TO HOLD AN AUDIENCE IN THE PALM OF YOUR HAND

PURPOSE

Once you have gained the favor of your audience, how can you use the first ingredient of the F.I.T.S. formula (favor) to create the second ingredient (interest)? In Step 2: Creating Interest, we focus on how to hold an audience in the palm of your hand, and how to beat out all the competing voices that vie for the interest of your audience. In this chapter we will consider how to:

1. make your audience want to hear what you have to say
2. move from acceptance to response
3. keep them begging for more

"Speech is the image of life."
—*Democritus*

NOW THAT I HAVE YOUR ATTENTION...

The tension was so thick you could cut it with a knife when I stepped to the microphone to address the top and middle management team of a large national corporation. For months there had been turmoil within the company—profits were down, and top management was determined to do whatever necessary to get them up.

Several key managers and a slew of middle managers had been fired, and massive realignment of duties had been announced the day before I arrived to talk about time management and productivity. The big question on everyone's mind was "Who's next to get the ax?"

Wow! What a moment to walk in!

Not only was I an outsider, most people in the audience assumed I had been called in by management to tell them what they had to do to keep their jobs. That made me a part of "them," and my task was to address those who thought of themselves as "us."

What do you do in a situation like that? What I always do is try to get back to basics and stay there, to stick with tested and proven principles and techniques.

By the time I finished my session with that group, they had dropped their mental barriers and invited me in. Perhaps even more amazingly, they were asking for more of my ideas. I had become part of their solution rather than part of their problem.

How did I do it? First, I spent extra time gaining their acceptance and favor. I sold myself, which is what I have talked about throughout the first section of this book. I then used their favor as a springboard for communicating my ideas to them, which is what this section of the book is all about.

You will find this chapter very useful, once you have learned how to sell yourself to an audience. But let me remind you that you cannot create interest in your ideas until you have taken the first step in the F.I.T.S. formula. You *must* gain the favor of your audience before they will listen to your ideas and concerns.

HOW TO MAKE PEOPLE WANT TO HEAR YOUR IDEAS

High-impact speakers are good company and interesting to be around. They make you feel special, like you're really somebody. They are interested in you, in what you do, in what you think, in how you feel.

Yes, they make you like them, but it's more that they make you like yourself or, at least, make you feel like you're worth something. Soon, they're making you want to be more than you are. It seems as if they accept you for what you are and invite you to go on with them to become more of what you can be.

By contrast, nobody likes to be around a bore. You probably know people like that. They only talk about themselves and their accomplishments. Or they talk about "great ideas" while you are thinking about great problems. Or maybe they want to talk about their problems while you try to think about great ideas. Most of all, they do not seem to care about your thoughts, feelings, or interests.

What's the difference? Why is it that you can't wait until some speakers finish while you wish others would keep going for hours?

The Response Factor

Like good conversationalists, good public speakers understand and utilize the response factor in communicating. They have the ability to connect with an audience and get that audience to connect with them.

In our last chapter, we talked about stage presence—that ability to cause an audience to sit up and take notice when you come on stage. It is that crucial capacity for selling yourself to an audience.

The response factor, however, moves to the next level of intimacy with the audience—creating interest in your ideas. It is the ability to make people care about what is important to you and to want to hear what you have to say about what you want to get across.

Look, for example, at Michael Jackson, who is one of the most popular performers in the nation. It's not just that he feels the music so deeply. The "cat" who "grooves" down the street with a "boom box" may feel the music just as deeply. But more than that, Michael Jackson has the ability to make the audience feel the music *with* him.

Winston Churchill did the same thing with his speeches and radio talks. He had the ability to get masses of people to join with him in "putting a stop to the international tyranny of Nazi imperialism." Franklin D. Roosevelt did the same thing with his "fireside chats."

How You Can Use The Response Factor

"Those are giants in their fields.... What about people like me who just want to be able to speak to small groups?" you might be thinking.

What made those people giants in their fields was that they mastered the art of getting people to pay attention to them, which is exactly what any of us will have to do if we want to speak with high impact.

Maybe you are not planning to become a musical performer, or a head of state, a television personality, or even a motivational speaker. But by studying the success strategies of the giants in those fields, you can become better at whatever you choose to do. So, let's look carefully at some of the principles they use to get people to respond to them.

Principle 1: Cultivate Audience Sensitivity

Poor speakers say what they think and do not concern themselves with how their audience responds to it. For them, it's enough that "It's the truth."

Mediocre speakers say what they think, and watch the way people respond to it. They want what they say to be warmly received and acted upon.

High-impact speakers concern themselves with what their audience is thinking and feeling. This involves much more than simply saying what you think people want to hear. In fact, some very high-impact speakers regularly say things their audiences would rather not hear, but they never run roughshod over the feelings of the people who are listening to them.

All of us have our own "circles of possibility" which we tend to protect from invaders who threaten us with new possibilities we have not yet considered. However, we tend to readily receive ideas from people who seem to care about us and come to us with good will.

If you think about it, the great speakers you have heard have probably all worked hard to cultivate audience sensitivity. For example, sharp speakers never talk down to an audience, or ignore the physical needs of those who come to hear them, or crack ethnic jokes that could offend people in the audience. They don't put people down, or try to make them look silly. They have a sense of humanity, a feeling for the human touch. They seek to know their audiences as persons.

It is this simple: If you want to boost your audience impact rating, you must practice becoming sensitive to people until it becomes a habit with you. You must become so aware of the response factor that you can close your eyes and "feel" the presence of your audience. Once you have become sensitive to your audience, you are ready for the next principle for improving your audience impact rating.

Principle 2: Cultivate Audience Awareness

Awareness and sensitivity are closely related, but they are not the same thing. Being sensitive is being responsive, being willing to observe and listen, and being open to the needs and desires of your audience. You might think of it as an attitude of openness toward your audience.

Awareness is more active in that it is an assertive and ongoing involvement with your audience that enables you to set the pace for the dialogue you want to occur. High-impact speakers are so aware of their audiences they can sense the slightest mood change. They can predict when interest will be at its peak, and they know when it is time to quit. This awareness gives them a feeling for timing, for pacing, and for moving in for the close.

The more aware you are of what is going on with your audience the better you can pace your use of humor, illustrations, and powerful statements for maximum impact. By cultivating audience awareness, you can usually predict quite accurately what impact certain messages and speaking tactics will produce. Therefore, you can adjust your strategies to communicate more effectively.

If you want to get a feeling for how this works, notice how a skilled speaker will anticipate what reactions a statement or action will raise in the minds of their audience. Notice the use of statements like: "Right now you're probably wondering..." or "Which raises the question..." or "As strange as that may seem...." It's almost as if they are reading the minds of their listeners and anticipating what thoughts they are triggering. Actually, what they are doing is practicing awareness of the reactions of their audience. There is nothing mystical about it. It's sheer skill.

I suggest that if you want to boost your audience impact, you should cultivate an awareness of what is happening with the people you want to impact upon.

Principle 3: Seek to Understand Your Audience

One of the most successful professional speakers ever was Frank Bettger. He had a very simple formula for success: "Show people what they want and how to get it, and they will move Heaven and earth to get it."

If you are sensitive to your audience and aware of their feelings, which enables you to understand your audience, that opens the door to greater audience impact.

For example, you are wasting your time and boring your audience when you try to answer questions people are not asking. Even worse, you are wasting opportunities to communicate with others—opportunities which may never come again.

High-impact speakers keep certain questions in their minds during all their speeches. It helps them understand their audiences.

1. *What do these people want out of life?* Understanding people includes knowing how they perceive their needs and what they think it would take to satisfy them. What motivates them? What motivates them to do the opposite of what you want them to do?

People sometimes call me a motivational speaker, but actually I cannot motivate anybody. People do things for their own reasons—not for mine, nor for yours, nor for anyone else's. Furthermore, there is no such thing as an "unmotivated" person. While your audience might not be motivated to do what you want them to do, or what someone else wants them to do, they are motivated to do what *they* want to do.

What you and I do is get in touch with what motivates them and channel their motivations along lines that are compatible with our goals for them. You can also help your audiences mobilize their resources to achieve the goals that matter to them.

2. *What are they afraid of?* Understanding people's fears can often help you focus their attention on what you have to say. In fact, there are times when creating interest requires the use of fears.

To illustrate: Before you can rescue a drowning person from the water, you must first overcome his or her terror at the prospect of dying. When you have convinced people that you can rescue them, they will relax and let you pull them to shore. On the other hand, if you are trying to stop someone who has been drinking from driving a car, appealing to the fear of death might be a very effective technique.

What is important to remember is that before you know how to deal with the fears of an audience, you must first understand what those fears are. The better you understand their fears, the more you can boost your audience impact rating.

3. *What do they know and understand?* Jargon can be a great help in establishing contact with certain audiences, and it can sometimes help you get right to the point. However, if your

audience does not understand your jargon, you will only confuse them and close the door to all communication.

As an old saying goes, "All you need to know to teach a dog how to do tricks, is more than the dog knows." Yet it is even more important to know what the dog knows.

What you understand very well, others may not understand at all. Once you are in touch with what people know and understand, you may move on to show them what they do not know or understand.

4. *What do they misunderstand?* The other side of the question can pose real problems when you are trying to create interest in your ideas.

The audience I mentioned at the beginning of this chapter grossly misunderstood my reasons for being there. Before I could get to first base with them, I had to clear up their misconception that I was called in by management to tell them what was expected of them.

By understanding them, I was able to convince them of my real motivations. Then they were interested in what I had to offer. The way I did it was to talk about some of the pressures I had felt back in my coaching days. I talked about how all the alumni wanted was for my teams to win, how the faculty and parents of the players wanted me to see to it that the kids got a good education, and how the administration was always yelling about saving money and getting fans to pay for tickets to the games.

Gradually, they began to see that I understood what it was to be under tremendous pressure, and they began to open up. It wasn't long before they were really interested in what worked for me.

When people misunderstand the information they are being given or the speaker's motivation for giving it, they will throw up an impenetrable wall of resistance. If you want people to become interested in your ideas, always stay alert for any misunderstanding and deal with it properly.

Principle 4: Identify With Your Audience

The father of two small boys was trying to catch up on some overdue reading when the kitchen suddenly erupted with angry shouts. Dropping his newspaper, he rushed out to see the boys about to come to blows over a piece of leftover pie.

At first, he tried to settle the argument by suggesting he cut the pie and flip a coin to see which of them had first choice. Since one of the boys felt he was unlucky, that idea was dropped quickly, as were several others. Finally, the father decided to try to look at things through the eyes of each of the boys. Almost instantly, he came up with a solution that both boys readily accepted.

"One of you can cut the pie, and the other will have first choice of the slices," the father proposed and the boys agreed. Soon the pie had been cut into two of the most perfectly equal pieces imaginable. The boys were satisfied, and the father was back at his reading.

It is amazing what seeing the world through the eyes of other people can do to change your perspective. It can give you valuable insights about how to create interest in your ideas. It is even more amazing how the more you identify with the circumstances, needs, and feelings of your audience, the easier it is for your audience to identify with you.

Notice, for example, how many times Abraham Lincoln used the pronoun "we" in the Gettysburg Address, to which we referred earlier. He wanted to make sure they knew he shared their grief and pain, so he talked about how "*our* forefathers brought forth a new nation," how "*we* are engaged in a great civil war," and how "*we* have come to dedicate...." As you read that speech, you could almost believe that the dead men were his brothers, or his sons, or his father.

If you contrast that with much of the political rhetoric today, it is easy to see why so many people are becoming alienated from our nation's leaders. They use terms like, "The American people are tired of...." or "Our polls show people want...." or "My record clearly shows...."

It is as if some speakers are afraid they will lose their own identity if they identify with the feelings and needs of their audiences. That is a rather insecure position.

Real dialog can only happen when you and your audience identify with each other. Insecure speakers tend to say, "Let me make my position absolutely clear to you." But high-impact speakers always try to identify with their audiences.

HOW TO MOVE FROM FAVOR TO RESPONSE

Think for a moment about your most successful attempt to communicate with other people. Maybe it was the first time you said "I love you" to a person who now occupies a significant place in your life. Perhaps it was a job interview that opened the door to a great opportunity for you. Or maybe you spoke to a large audience and felt them breathing with you.

Whatever comes to mind as a high moment in your communication experience, one thing is certain: it was a moment when you experienced response from your audience, whether that audience was made up of one or 1,000. And undoubtedly you would like to experience greater response more often from your audiences.

How can you increase the frequency with which you really connect with your audiences? Let's look at some tested and proven tactics which can help you move from favor to response.

Response Tactic 1: Get Your Audience Physically Involved With You

The quickest and most effective way to make your audience responsive is to get them to do things with you. Even when strong barriers exist, they can be broken down by either getting the whole audience to do something, or calling an individual up front to do something before the whole crowd.

You can, for example, ask for a show of hands on a humorous question. The results can sometimes be hilarious. I once asked how many of the men present dominated their wives. Only one guy raised his hand. That brought a big laugh. But what really brought the house down was his wife, who stood up and pushed his arm down. After playing with it a little while, I used that incident as a springboard to make the point that time moves on, and we must keep pace with it. I had their interest from that moment on.

Another involvement trick many speakers use very effectively is calling someone up from the audience to get them to do something. This is powerful because when you involve one person from the audience, the whole audience identifies with that person, particularly if it is a person who is known by everybody in the group. It's a trick pioneered by magicians, who would often call for a volunteer from the audience. Instant credibility! Those masters of the stage obviously knew more about creating interest and connecting than simply pulling rabbits out of hats.

Here are some tips on involving your audience:

1. Keep it simple.
2. Make it move.
3. Keep it short.
4. Make it fun for everyone.
5. Make it fit your audience and the situation.
6. Make certain you do not embarrass anyone.
7. Make sincere compliments for all who participate a big part of your routine.
8. Make the audience applaud anyone who comes up front.

When you get the whole audience involved, it makes each individual feel good, and identifies you as one of the crowd.

Most professional speakers develop their own exercises for getting people involved with them because they want to find tactics that fit their own personalities and styles. However, there are several good books available at your local library which contain many exercises you can adapt.

Response Tactic 2: Animate Your Whole Presentation

Abraham Lincoln, who evidently knew a great deal about animating presentations, often commented about one specific type of public speaker—the preacher.

"I don't like to hear cut-and-dried sermons," said Abe. "When I hear a man preach I like to see him act as if he were fighting bees."

Now that's an animated presentation!

Remember, everything you say, and everything you do communicates something to your audience. Spaghetti-like arms hanging down your sides tell your audience you are scared to death. If your arms are folded rigidly across your chest, it says to the audience that you are defensive. Hands nervously fidgeting with glasses or notes communicate extreme self-consciousness.

Relax and get into what you are saying, then your audience will also relax and get into what you are saying. Nothing communicates like enthusiasm; and nothing conveys enthusiasm like animation. Your audience can tell how strongly you believe what you are saying by observing the tone of your voice, your expression, and your gestures.

Practice saying things expressively. Practice using gestures to good advantage and handling a microphone until you can do it naturally without making it pop. Practice, practice, practice, and you can become a very animated speaker, even if you are naturally shy.

Then, when you are before an audience, let yourself go! Let all of the power of your personality come through. Your audience may not become as animated as you would like, but they will never become more animated than you do.

Response Tactic 3: Accent with Visuals

Television has helped to make us a very visually oriented society. Experts say that 85 percent of what we learn comes through our eyes. That suggests two very important considerations for a person who would seek to become a high-impact speaker.

First, it means there is tremendous power in visual communications. If you can present your ideas visually as well as verbally, your impact will take a quantum leap.

Second, it means that most distractions are visual. To create and sustain interest in what you have to say, you must give your audience something to watch, as well as something to hear.

Earlier, I told you how you could use elements in your environment to create visual interest. Remember the story about the real estate salesman who sold a blossoming cherry tree, and threw in the house as a bonus? It's a strategy I strongly recommend.

But you can also use prepared visuals to great advantage, provided you do it well. Here are some pointers on powerful visuals:

1. Keep them simple and their use short.
2. Send only one message per visual.
3. Use visuals which create interest in your message, rather than in themselves. For example, a picture of a nude body might create interest, but not necessarily in your ideas.
4. Practice showing all visuals until you can do it comfortably.
5. Check to be sure everything works before the presentation begins, and be prepared for malfunctions. For instance, I always carry extra bulbs for projectors.
6. Apply the visuals to what you are saying.

If you will plan carefully and use them wisely, visuals can greatly help you to gain the interest of your audience.

HOW TO KEEP THEM BEGGING FOR MORE

Ideas become interesting to us only when they become very personal. The implication for the public speaker is clear: Get personal, gain attention.

Let me illustrate. When someone yells "Fire!" what's the first thing you ask? "Where?" You want to know how close that fire is to you. The farther removed it is from you and from your concerns, the less important it becomes to you.

For example, you might be keenly interested in watching a news bulletin about a fire in your neighborhood, especially if arson is suspected. But, if there is a report of a forest fire thousands of miles away, you would probably only shake your head in compassion for the victims and continue with what you were doing.

If you want to gain and hold the interest of your audience, nothing helps like keeping the focus on the personal needs, desires, and concerns of the people you want to interest. It's the best way I know to keep them begging for more. I will have more to say about this vital point further along in the book.

SO, WHAT HAVE WE SAID?

Success at public speaking comes from getting people to respond to you and your ideas. It is what I call your audience impact rating, and it is the measure of your ability to get people interested in what you have to say.

As a speaker, your most pressing task is to create and sustain the interest of your audience. To do that you must cultivate the audience's sensitivity, awareness, and understanding, and be able to identify with your audience.

In short, if you will show enough interest in your audience, you can interest them in what you have to say.

ACTION STEPS

1. Try to remember a time when a speaker or individual captured your interest in a subject you normally would not care much about. Then try to analyze how that person captured your imagination.

2. Think of specific ways you can use the ideas of this chapter in your own public speaking.

HOW TO HOLD INTEREST

PURPOSE

High-impact public speakers realize they always have stiff competition for the interest of their audiences, and they rely on proven strategies to hold interest—no matter what happens. This chapter will focus on:

1. how to utilize all your speaking skills to hold a high-interest level
2. how to handle distractions and interruptions effectively

"He that wrestles with us . . . sharpens our skills. Our antagonist is our helper."

—*Burke*

MAY I HAVE YOUR ATTENTION, PLEASE?

We all face competition every time we speak, whether we are speaking to a handful of business associates or an audience of thousands.

For instance, Kinney Shoe Corporation had invited me to do a seminar in Corpus Christi, Texas. My speech was going well. I was talking about crisis management, and I had just made a strong statement that the most important thing to remember during a crisis is not to overreact.

Just as I made that statement, a fire alarm went off. There was a big round of laughter, then we all carefully filed out of the room. Once we were safely outside, I got some good-natured ribbing about how some people would go to any lengths to make a point. Later, I discussed how staying cool in a crisis enables you to make the best of a bad situation. To this day, some of those people may think I arranged for that fire alarm to go off at just the right moment.

Let me assure you that not all my competition has worked to my advantage so beautifully. More often than not I, like most speakers, have had to work very hard to keep the interest of my audience when a major distraction or disturbance has arisen.

In this chapter, I will share some of the principles and techniques that have worked well for me in dealing with competition.

UTILIZE ALL YOUR SPEAKING SKILLS

The greatest test of a speaker's skills is what he or she does when something unscheduled happens. It is then that the amateurs start squirming, but those who have adequately prepared themselves face up to it and try to turn it to their advantage.

Let's look at some tested and proven principles which can help you head off disasters and deal effectively with them when they do arise.

Principle 1: Plan To Prevent Problems

Nothing can weaken a speaker's impact quite as much as going in unprepared, or even looking unprepared. It destroys your self-confidence, and it can disorient you and make you fumble. Being unprepared can cause you to make mistakes you would not otherwise make.

Perhaps even worse, it makes you look bad in the eyes of the audience. It's hard to take control when everyone present is chuckling at your bumbling attempts to get your act together.

Planning to prevent problems includes:

1. Knowing precisely what you plan to do the whole time you are in front of the group. You may have to change your plan, but changing horses in the middle of a race is much easier than racing with no horse at all.
2. Having all your equipment and aids ready. Not having the proper equipment, not having equipment in working order, or not having visuals organized will quickly lose the interest of your audience.
3. Understanding the needs, desires, and expectations of your audience. It is inexcusable, for example, not to know in advance such things as the demographic make-up of your audience, what they expect from you, and what time you should be through.
4. Planning to arrive early enough to get your bearings. Rushing in late, or at the last minute, is inviting disaster and creating unnecessary tension.

Even if you have a standard speech or program you do over and over again, it is quite possible to overlook one or more of the areas I have mentioned. If you do, you can count on damaging or even destroying the interest of your group.

The Boy Scouts are right: "Always be prepared!" To do so is to head off most of the disasters unprepared speakers bring upon themselves.

Principle 2: Plan To Deal With Disasters

As some of my younger friends say, "stuff happens." No matter how carefully you plan, things can and often do go wrong.

For example, one of my friends was just building up to his dramatic closing story, when all the lights suddenly went out—even the exit lights. Now, that's a disaster! Oddly enough, his p.a. system kept working. Fortunately, he had planned ahead for such problems and was able to make the most of it.

"We don't realize what a blessing electricity is to us until something like this comes along, do we?" he said. "But while we wait for the staff to get the lights back on, let me tell you about a woman named Helen Keller who lived in a world as dark as the room we're in right now. Imagine how she must have felt when. . . ." Then he told how this magnificent woman conquered overwhelming problems to become one of the truly great people of history.

While it was not the story he had planned to use, he had held it in reserve for just such a time as this. It worked beautifully.

Here are some pointers on how to plan for disasters:

1. Plan to stay cool—no matter what happens. Panic always makes a problem worse, but almost no problem is insurmountable if you stay calm and think about how to react to it.
2. Keep going if you can. You may have to acknowledge the problem, but you seldom have to give in to it. Meeting planners will greatly appreciate it if you can keep things moving while they try to correct the problem.
3. Keep the crowd calm and together. When you take control, you also assume responsibility for the well-being of the audience. Your calm, assuring manner can do wonders to break the tension.
4. Develop and memorize a strong set of contingency plans. Ask: "What would I do if the lights went out, the mike went dead, a projector bulb blew, there was a sudden unexplained noise, or whatever." Include in your plans what you would do without notes, without visuals, or other equipment. That is not being a prophet of doom, it's being ready.

By planning ahead, you can very often turn a disaster into a triumph.

Principle 3: Avoid Competing With Yourself

Some speakers actually create their own competition.

Have you ever watched nervously while the person up front twirled a pair of eyeglasses the whole time he or she was talking? You cannot concentrate on what such a person is saying for watching those endangered glasses.

Such things as stopping periodically to take a sip of water, coughing or snickering nervously, or constantly referring to your notes can cause your audience to lose interest in a hurry.

Another common form of self-created competition is displaying bad verbal habits. The speaker who continually repeats meaningless words like "you know" or "uhhh" often finds audience members counting how many time such expressions come up, instead of listening with great interest to what is being said. That's why it is so important to practice with the aid of a cassette player. You might sometimes want to crawl under a rock after hearing yourself, but it's better than continuing to make the same mistakes over and over without knowing it.

Reading a speech is another way of inviting the competition to capture the interest of your audience, for several important reasons. First, most audiences react negatively to it. They wonder why you don't simply make copies of your speech and send them out, instead of assembling the group.

Second, good speech writing is a special art which only relatively few people can do well. If you read something, it had better be extraordinarily well written.

Third, oral reading is actually much more difficult to do well than is speaking from prepared remarks. Even professional narrators practice a great deal before they record. Then they have sound engineers edit all their bloopers.

It is always better to study your speech well enough so that it sounds extemporaneous. If you feel you must read it, by all means practice it until you can read it well.

There is always enough competition to contend with, without creating more for yourself. Sometimes it is helpful to ask pointed questions of trusted critics to find out what distractions you create habitually. It may be painful to find out, but it beats continuing to make them.

Principle 4: Stay Alert For Audience Distraction

Being sensitive and aware of your audience at all times is something we have considered before. However, it is particularly important in eliminating the distractions that vie for the interest of your audience.

It is this factor that makes advance preparation and practice so crucial. If you are composing your talk as you go along, or constantly looking at a text or notes, you will not have the presence of mind to monitor the audience to see if they are being distracted by competition.

A slight change in the response level of your audience will often be your first signal that something is drawing their interest away from you. The following pointers can help you stay on top of any indication that your audience is losing interest:

1. *Watch your audience.* Observe everything your audience does, watching for any symptom of wandering interest or difficulty in following you. Look for signs that people in the back of the room are having problems hearing you clearly. Pause periodically to see that everyone has a clear view of you and anything you want them to see, and correct problems before you proceed.

If people who were sitting alertly and maintaining eye contact with you are beginning to slump in their chairs, or if their eyes have begun to rove, it often indicates that the room is becoming uncomfortable. Always pin down the source of the problem before you lose them completely. Stay alert for such problems as people sitting too long in one position, needing to go to the restroom, or struggling with uncomfortable chairs. A stand-up exercise or a short break can often rescue a speech that is giving way to the competition of fatigue or discomfort.

2. *Monitor audience resistance.* You will sometimes find that the audience resists what you have to say because of emotional or intellectual factors.

Let's say you are called upon to give a report that is unpopular for some reason. It is information you must give, but information the audience does not want to receive. They might start challenging your statistics or questioning your facts. More likely, they will simply tune you out and sit passively and inattentively.

By recognizing the problem and coming up with strategies for dealing with it, you can at least get your message across. You might even succeed in changing their minds. However, if you do not recognize the resistance, you might assume you have done very well, only to find out later they didn't hear a word you said. Such situations are tough to deal with, but they are even worse when you try to pretend they do not exist.

Sensitivity is the key to monitoring audience resistance, but there are techniques that can help you with the monitoring process.

First, listen to the audience response. When emotional or intellectual resistance is present, you can spot it immediately by the way the audience responds to your one-liners and stories. Audience response is to the public speaker what symptoms are to a doctor. The sensitive speaker knows what kind of response to expect and, when that response is not forthcoming, he or she seeks to determine why.

Second, check your audience impact rating by testing the waters periodically to see if the audience is resisting or receiving the messages you are sending. You not only want to know if the audience is backing away from you, you want to know if it is grasping the messages you are trying to get across. You can find out by asking a question that the audience can answer with one word. If they shout back the answer, you know you're getting through. If only a few people respond, check further to see if you are losing your audience. The high-impact speaker knows what response is desired and constantly checks to see that the desired response is building up through the whole talk.

3. *Custom fit your style to your audience.* Obviously, you

have to use a little common sense in making your presentations. It would not be appropriate for a minister to get his audience involved in a clapping game at a funeral, nor would you involve a group of physically handicapped people in vigorous exercises.

Skilled speakers give you the feeling that everything they say is meant for your ears alone, that you matter more than anyone in the world at that moment, and what they have to say to you is of vital importance. That is their way of beating out the competition.

DEAL EFFECTIVELY WITH DISTRACTIONS AND INTERRUPTIONS

When you speak in public, you have to expect distractions. If you are speaking in a public meeting place, the distractions might be the clatter of dishes from an adjoining area, or noises from down the hall, or people wandering in and out. Sometimes, just the experience of being in a strange place can cause interest to wander.

If you are speaking to a small group of business associates, distractions might include phone calls coming in, or someone interrupting you, or a strong attraction outside a window or door.

Recently, I was speaking to an audience of about 1,000 people and things were moving along well. Suddenly, the microphone started picking up messages from the local police station and broadcasting them loudly and clearly.

When those things come up, you need to have strategies for dealing with them and contingency plans for holding interest. Let's look at some things you can do.

Strategy 1: Know What You Are Getting Into

One of the most difficult challenges I have ever faced as a speaker was when I had to share a program for 1,200 people with Dr. Norman Vincent Peale. However, I was able to cope with that situation because I had done my homework and knew exactly what I was facing before I went into that auditorium. But, occasionally, I let a programming situation slip up on me, and have to fight to keep the interest of my group.

For example, a large association hired me to do a time management and productivity seminar. When I saw that I was scheduled as the closing feature of a long convention, it should have alerted me that trouble was brewing. However, I was so excited about the invitation that I did not check out what I was getting into. To make matters worse, my seminar was scheduled for Friday afternoon. As I later discovered, the association members traditionally leave early on Friday afternoon because they face three to five hours of commuting.

When I started speaking, the response was great. But by the end of the first break, about a third of my audience was gone. By midafternoon, nearly half the people were gone, and by the time I finished, about 3:45 PM, only 20 percent of the people were left. It was one of the very few times in all my years of speaking that I have ever had people walk out on me. I was crushed!

Oddly enough, the meeting planner came rushing up to me after the meeting and was very pleased. "Imagine," he said, "what would have happened if we didn't have somebody who could hold the audience!"

The point is that I should have known about the traditional emptying auditorium before I went in. I could have suggested alternatives in scheduling or some format changes which could have helped me hold interest against such overwhelming competition. I resolved that day always to do a better job of research about where I fit into a program before I go in to speak. The best time to deal with such problems is in the planning stages—before potential competition becomes a real problem.

Strategy 2: Clear Away Environmental Distractions

Many speakers are doomed to failure at the start because of factors in the environment that compete for their interest. High-impact speakers know that there are certain conditions that are difficult to cope with, and they have learned to work closely with meeting planners to try to eliminate them before a session begins.

There are at least five built-in environmental distractions you should be alert for and deal with before your speech begins.

BUILT-IN DISTRACTION 1:
AN UNSUITABLE LOCATION

How much competition you will have can often be determined by the size, shape, and location of the room in which you speak. A room that is too large, for instance, can create a space barrier between you and your audience which makes eye contact impossible and allows for distractions from other sources. On the other hand, a room that is too small can make people uncomfortable and give them a feeling of being packed in. Add the smoke of a few inconsiderate people to a crowded room, and you have major competition.

Some rooms also have poor acoustics. If you turn down the public address system, the audience cannot hear you; if you turn it up, the sound echoes as if you were in a barrel.

If you can do so, suggest a room tailored to the size of the group and fitted acoustically to the speaking activity. Before you speak, monitor the environment and make plans to deal with any competition it creates. To ignore the environment is to surrender to the competition.

BUILT-IN DISTRACTION 2: AN UNCOMFORTABLE ROOM

Interest in what you have to say can be damaged, or even destroyed, by the temperature or lighting of a room. If you try to speak in a room that is too warm or dimly lit, your audience will become drowsy, listless, and inattentive. Competition might even include snores, if the conditions are bad enough.

A room that is too cool, on the other hand, can make an audience restless and inattentive. Too much lighting can destroy the feeling of intimacy you are seeking to create. Such conditions can make your audience tense.

Always check your room temperature and lighting conditions before you stand up to speak, for two important reasons: (1) when you stand to speak, you will have enough on your mind without having to worry about the thermostat and light level; (2) as you speak, your activity and intensity will naturally make you warmer than your audience.

If, at any time during your speech, you sense that your audience is physically uncomfortable, stop and try to correct the problem. Otherwise, you will lose out to the competition.

BUILT-IN DISTRACTION 3: EQUIPMENT PROBLEMS

Balky or inadequate public address systems, projectors that don't work properly, or easels that will not stand up can give almost any speaker more competition than he or she can handle.

It is a good idea to arrive early enough to check out all equipment you will be using and to eliminate any problems you find—before the program begins. It also helps to talk with the person who will be operating the equipment to make sure he or she understands your needs and wishes. If a problem arises while you are speaking, always remember that it is a solution you should seek—not someone to blame.

BUILT-IN DISTRACTION 4: VISUAL DISTRACTIONS

A large company once invited me to speak to their sales force at a convention in a resort hotel. The problem was that the meeting room had an open view of the swimming pool, filled with people in bathing suits enjoying themselves. While I think I am a good speaker, nobody is good enough to hold the interest of an audience with competition like that!

The room itself often contains distractions. If you speak often, you will find competition from waiters clearing tables or serving food, people getting up and wandering around, people taking pictures with flashbulbs and many other actions that compete for the attention of the audience.

Check the room in advance, and eliminate any visual distractions you can. If you cannot eliminate them, at least come up with a strategy for overcoming them. When distractions occur during your speech, it is usually better to stop until they are dealt with, and then move on.

BUILT-IN DISTRACTION 5: UNCONTROLLED NOISES

Noises sometimes seem to come from everywhere and at the worst possible times. You may get competition from jackhammers breaking up concrete, kitchen workers, other meetings or parties, airplanes flying low overhead, and many other sources.

Often the competition comes from sounds that are not unpleasant, and in fact, that's the problem. They are so interesting that they draw the audience away from you. For example, music from an adjoining room can be very distracting. To keep your speech from being drowned out by noises and distracting sounds, you will need to do everything you can to eliminate or outperform them.

Monitoring the environment is one of the most challenging tasks of any public speaker. But if you approach that task creatively, you will be amazed at how many of the competing distractions you can eliminate. If you cannot eliminate them, you must develop strategies for dealing with them. Simply to ignore them is to give up and let the competing voices have the interest of your audience.

Strategy 3: Avoid Overreacting

Dealing with distractions and interruptions can be demanding because, in speaking, most of the pressure is in your own mind. Your expectations will almost always be higher than those of your audience; and indeed they should be. After all, you want always to do your very best. It is part of what gives you high impact as a speaker.

However, high personal expectations can be hazardous to your perspective. They can cause you to overreact to interruptions—even those you can do nothing about.

I was speaking recently in a big auditorium, filled with about 1,500 people. Early in my speech I noticed a slight smell of gas, and it seemed to grow worse as time progressed. Soon everybody in the audience could smell it, so I could not just ignore it and hope it would go away quickly. Besides, a gas leak is potentially dangerous.

The meeting chairman signaled me to continue while the maintenance people tried to find and fix the problem. Meanwhile, the audience and I were growing more tense by the moment.

Suddenly, I realized that I had an audience and a speech to think about, while there were qualified people who could concentrate totally on fixing the leak and evacuating the auditorium, if that became necessary. My task was to keep the interest of the audience.

Since my speech had been interrupted, I knew that the best thing I could do was to try to entertain the people as best I could until the problem was solved. At last, I received the signal that the problem had been corrected, and announced to the audience that the crisis was over. Then I went back and picked up my speech.

By not overreacting, I managed to salvage a speech which appeared at one point to be hopelessly lost. That experience taught me two lessons: (1) most crises appear more threatening than they really are, and (2) losing the interest of your audience makes the problem even worse.

Strategy 4: Make It Funny

A good sense of humor can be one of the greatest assets a public speaker can have, especially when you are interrupted.

The natural thing to do when your speech is disrupted is to get angry, lose your temper, and let someone have the full fury of your wrath. That is particularly true in the case of hecklers. But you are always miles ahead of the game if you can keep your cool and try to make the situation funny. It is also a good idea to avoid embarrassing or humiliating anybody.

Let me explain by using an illustration. Lately, it seems that I have had a rash of "misplaced persons" when speaking at conventions. Those are folks who wander in and take a seat (usually right down front), only to jump up after I have been speaking for a few minutes and say "I must be in the wrong room!"

Frankly, I find that more than a little irritating. And I have seen speakers try to make fools of such people as they exit. That can be a big mistake, for several reasons:

1. Audiences generally identify more with other members of the audience than they do with speakers, especially in the early stages of a speech. To jump on a person is to come down on the wrong side and can make your audience angry and mistrustful of you.
2. Most people feel a natural empathy with a person who must publicly admit a mistake. They may take your attack on the "lost soul" as a personal affront.
3. Nobody likes to see another person publicly humiliated, unless the offender clearly has it coming. Attacking such a person can make you look like a *prima donna*.
4. By lowering the boom, you miss out on a golden opportunity to show your audience what a warm and clever person you are. If you can identify with the disrupter in a humorous way, you can endear yourself to the audience and set a warm, friendly atmosphere that will help everyone relax and trust you. That is too good an opportunity to pass up.

The best rule of thumb in handling disruptions is to always put yourself in the position of the audience. If the disruption is annoying them, deal with it forthrightly and quickly; if it's not bothering them, either let it go or make a joke out of it.

Let's look back at the guidelines I gave you earlier for handling hecklers. I said that on the first round, I deal with them very gently and try to pass it off with a joke. That's because I have learned that audiences tend to identify with hecklers at first, and are at least mildly amused that the hecklers are invading my turf.

On the second round, I usually get a little tougher with them and exert strong control. I have learned that by the second time around, most people in the audience are getting a little put out with the hecklers because they have begun to feel the hecklers are invading *their* turf.

But on the third round, I lower the boom on hecklers, because by then most people in the audience are beginning to get very irate with them. They might even begin to get angry with me for letting such people take over their meeting.

Whatever happens, keep your sense of humor intact and try to make even the worst situations funny. And, by all means, use great tact when dealing with disruptive people. As long as the audience is laughing with you, they are not laughing at you.

SO, WHAT HAVE WE SAID?

If you speak in public, you will have competition—you can count on it! So it is best to expect it, to work hard to prevent it, and always to have strong strategies for dealing with it. It is the only way you can hold the interest of your audience.

Moreover, by always being well prepared and facing every competing force, you can actually strengthen your own skills as a public speaker. If dealing with distractions and disruptions makes you better at what you do, they can't be all bad, can they?

ACTION STEPS

1. Reflect upon a speech you have heard in which the speaker had to fight for the interest of the audience. If the speaker managed to hold interest, analyze why. If the interest of the audience was lost, explore how it could have been saved by using the strategies and techniques we have discussed in this chapter.

2. List some ways you can improve your own batting average at holding interest, based on what you have read.

STARTING AT THE BACK END— WITH RESULTS

PURPOSE

We have seen how crucial it is to gain favor (Step 1) and to create interest (Step 2). Now we are ready to discover how vital it is to get your message across. That brings us to Step 3 of the F.I.T.S. formula for high impact public speaking: conveying a thought. We will discover why and how you need to start at the back end, with the results you wish to achieve, and how to prepare and present a speech that is clear, powerful, and persuasive.

Since most of the readers of this book are or will be in business or public life, we can assume that when you speak you want to get results. You want people to act: to do something, to buy something, or maybe just to understand important information. Thus, Chapter 7 will suggest that you take a results approach by concentrating on:

1. knowing specifically what you want to accomplish
2. making your message fit your audience's purpose
3. pulling it all together into a clearly targeted message

> "I have always thought the greatest symbol of common sense was building a bridge."
> —*Franklin D. Roosevelt*

MAKING THE MOST OF PRIME TIME

Have you ever noticed how the major television networks guard the hours from eight to eleven each night! They know that is when they have their largest audiences and, therefore, when they can make the most money by selling commercials. They call it *prime time*.

As a public speaker, your prime time is the precious few minutes when you are standing before an audience, actually conveying your ideas. It is that opportunity that comes rarely (sometimes once in a lifetime) to sell yourself and your ideas to those who are important to you. Even if you speak fairly frequently, you probably guard your prime time with a passion.

Maybe you have a chance to make a group sales presentation to the decision makers of a prospective buyer, and you want to make a sale. Perhaps you have a chance to better your position with your own company or within your career field. It could be that your organization is facing a great challenge which will require peak performance from all your coworkers, and you want to inspire them to act.

You know that a good speech can get you what you want, perhaps better than any other vehicle. Yet it is that very desire to make the most of every opportunity that creates tremendous pressure for public speakers.

It is also the same driving force which creates pressure to fall into the most frequent trap of speakers—trying to say too much, in too short a time.

A statement like "My time is almost gone, but I've scarcely scratched the surface of what I want to say" is a frequently heard indication that a speaker has fallen into the trap. Another is when a speaker announces at the beginning of a speech that he or she has fifteen points to cover, then thirty minutes later says "My second point is . . . ."

The key to giving a high-impact speech—one that produces the response you desire—is deciding in advance what you are going to do and how you are going to do it, then allocating the time needed to get it done. And, of course, following precisely the plan you have made.

In this chapter I will show you how to prepare and present a clearly focused message with the appropriate impact, a message which is easy for your audience to follow and to recall later.

ASKING THE MOST CRUCIAL, BUT LEAST ASKED, QUESTION

Wendell Phillips, the great orator, had given a lecture in Chicago and had been warmly received by his audience. Yet when Henry Ward Beecher, who had attended, later went to see his friend Phillips, he found him uneasy and dissatisfied with the lecture he had given.

Finally Phillips said: "I know what the matter was. It was only a speech. I was not fighting for any needy cause; I was not defending any great truth. It was just words, words, words."

Almost everyone present at that speech had admired it, but Wendell Phillips knew better. He knew that he had not accomplished what he had set out to do.

Quite likely, the reason he failed to accomplish his goal is that he had not asked himself the most crucial question a speaker can ask: "Why should I make this speech?"

As simple and basic as that question seems, it is the one least asked by public speakers. They fail to ask it (or at least to answer it satisfactorily) of themselves, of those who invited them, and of the audience. As a result, what they end up with are "just words, words, words."

If you were to stop most speakers on their way to the dais and ask them why they are going to make their speech, you would probably get answers like these:

"I was invited to speak!"
"I don't know why I was invited to speak!"
"I've got some things I want to get off my chest!"
"I was roped into it!"
"I don't know how I get into messes like this!"

Some speakers will even say such things in their opening remarks to an audience, then wonder why the audience pays so little attention to them. What a waste of opportunities!

Knowing specifically what you want to accomplish is the most crucial factor in getting an audience to do what you want them to do. Your purpose may be to entertain, it may be to motivate, to inform, to educate, to inspire. It may be to provoke thought, to calm ruffled feathers, or to do a host of other things. Whatever your aim may be, it is absolutely vital that your objective be focused clearly.

It's A Multidimensional Question

"Why make this speech?" is a question with several important dimensions. It implies questions like:

—Why should I be the person to make this speech?
—Why should I speak to this group?
—Why should I speak at this time?
—Why would this group listen to my message?

Good speeches occur when the right person says the right thing, to the right people, at the right place at the right time, and in the right way to be heard and understood and produce the desired response.

It is this simple: If you do not know what you want, how can you get it?

Set Specific Objectives For Each Speech

High-impact speakers always start at the end—with the results they wish to achieve—and work forward. Once they know clearly what they want, they are in a position to determine what they must do to get it.

Setting specific objectives for a speech may not be as easy as it sounds. For example, if you are making a group sales presentation, it may sound simple to say your ultimate goal is to make a sale. That may not, however, be a valid objective for this presentation. It may be that all you can hope to accomplish with this presentation is to convince the decision makers that your firm is reliable and should be allowed to bid against others they are considering. If you try too hard to make a one-shot sale, you might easily spend all your time answering questions they are not yet asking.

The best way to set specific goals and objectives for each speech is to ask yourself very pointed, results-oriented questions. Let me show you how asking yourself the right questions can lead to the results you want.

Ask yourself, what if my audience did precisely what I wish them to do? What would that be, and how would I know that they did it? Before you answer those questions too quickly, consider what they mean. Let's say you have a great idea you want to present to the management of a group you represent. You present that idea in a speech you have carefully prepared and skillfully deliver. When you finish, the audience compliments you with statements like "Brilliant speech!" and "Great idea!" However, a year later, you notice that nothing has been done to implement the idea.

If your objective was to make a good speech, it is clear that you have succeeded; but if your objective was to get the group to implement the idea, you would have to say that you were less than successful. "The operation was a success, but the patient died." Anyone who has a flair for showmanship can make a speech that will draw applause and compliments, but a high-impact speaker can give speeches which make things happen.

"I felt as if I wanted to rush right out and do something big," said a friend of mine after hearing a strong motivational talk, "but I didn't have the vaguest idea what!" If the speaker's objective was to generate a lot of excitement, he had succeeded. But if the objective was to get my friend to do something important, he had failed.

It reminds me of the fellow who fell in love and wanted his sweetheart to marry him. Since he was rather timid, he sent her a card every day for a year, and then he planned to ask for her hand in marriage. Sure enough, at the end of a year of getting a beautiful card each day when the postman came, she got married—to the postman! The fellow had gotten a response, but it was not the one he desired.

One of the most frequent reasons audiences fail to respond in the desired way is that it is never made clear to them what response is desired. And the most frequent reason it is not made clear to the audience is that it is not clear to the speaker.

In a nutshell, what I am saying is that if desired results are not programmed into your speech they will not happen. And unless you know specifically what results you want, you cannot possibly program them in.

I have found it most helpful before each speech to write my specific objective, in a succinct sentence, before I begin preparing what I want to say. I strongly recommend it to you. It is only when you can state specifically what you want to accomplish that you can move to the next task in conveying your thoughts.

MAKING YOUR MESSAGE FIT YOUR AUDIENCE'S PURPOSE

"It is altogether fitting and proper that we do this," said Abraham Lincoln in his legendary Gettysburg Address. Even though Mr. Lincoln had to admit that "the brave men, living and dead," had already done by their deeds a much better job than a mere speaker could do, his speech was a perfect fit with his subject and audience.

Remember, good speeches occur when the right person says the right thing, to the right people, at the right place, at the right time, and in the right way to be heard and understood, and to produce the desired response. But how can you always make sure that happens when you speak? How can you always make your message fit your purpose, the occasion, the audience, and yourself?

Let me remind you of William James' famous statement: "That which is most personal is most interesting." What that means to you is that to be effective at public speaking, you must always have a clearly targeted message that is vitally interesting to your audience at that precise moment.

Broadcasting On Clear Channel WII–FM

It is not only vital to know what you want to accomplish, but you must know what your audience wants. Every person, in every audience you will ever speak to, will always be asking one simple question: "What's in it for me?"

Whether or not you agree that is as it should be, you would be making a mistake not to recognize that it's the way it really is. People have their inner radios tuned to one station alone, WII–FM (What's In It For Me?).

If you doubt it, ask yourself what you look for when you listen to a speech. You might think hearing a travelogue on Hawaii would be a complete waste of time—unless you have just won a free Hawaiian trip and are excited about going there.

One of the most helpful techniques I have learned about targeting my message to the purpose of my audience came from my experience with "crossed-hair" sighting devices during my Army officer's training. They use them on sophisticated weapons which can shoot further than the human eye can see clearly, and they can help you hit the smallest of targets from a great distance. You simply move the weapon into the position where the target is located precisely at the spot the two perpendicular lines (hairs) cross, then shoot.

To use the "crossed-hair" principle of targeting your messages, think of one line as representing your purpose and the other line as representing the purpose of your audience. The precise spot where your purpose and their purpose comes together is the perfect place to target your message.

"You can get everything you want in life if you help enough

other people get what they want," says Zig Ziglar, one of America's great speakers.[1]

How To Zero In On What Your Inviter Wants

The first essential step in finding out what your audience wants from you is finding out why the invitation has been extended.

A person who asks you to speak to a civic club might have only one purpose in mind for inviting you—to fill up the program schedule. Or that person might have a hidden agenda for your program, an agenda which might put you in hot water with the audience.

I often receive calls, for example, from people who say something like: "My people seem to waste a lot of time; I want you to come and talk to them about time management."

That may mean, "I want you to come down here and build a fire under them to motivate them to quit wasting time." Or, it could mean, "My people are all dedicated workers, but they need some help managing their time." It could also mean a number of other things.

My first objective in a situation like that is to find out the intended purpose of the person making the invitation. So, I have learned to ask pointed questions, such as:

- How would you describe your organization?
- What type of meeting is this?
- What are the basic objectives of this meeting?
- What specific responsibilities are you giving the speaker on this occasion?
- How much time do you want me to take?
- How do you feel this time could best be used?
- What other presentations will appear before or after my speech? How do they tie together? What basic themes do they share?
- What can you tell me about this audience and occasion which will help me personalize and improve my presentation, for the benefit of everyone involved?

Asking such questions is a lot more productive than simply saying, "Okay, tell me a little about the group."

Often, I find that the inviting person has only a fuzzy idea of the purpose for inviting me. If so, I can help that person crystallize

---

[1] Zig Ziglar, *See You At The Top* (Gretna, LA: Pelican, 1977), p. 40. Copyright 1975, 1977, by Zig Ziglar.

the objectives for the meeting. You would be amazed at how much help that can be in targeting your message for a specific audience.

How To Zero In On What Your Audience Wants

Admittedly, it is not always easy to find out specifically what an audience wants from you as a speaker. One key reason is that the objectives of the audience are often quite different from those of the person who invites you to speak.

As a professional speaker, I always try to go beyond simply asking questions of the inviter. If possible, I go directly to members of the audience themselves. I have prepared some questionnaires, containing specific questions, which I send to a random sampling of people who will comprise the audience. That way I know precisely what the purpose of that group is in coming to hear me speak and can target my message accordingly.

Using a formal questionnaire may not always be convenient or even possible for you to do. But, whatever you have to do, find out as specifically as you can what that audience wants most from you. It is the surest way I know to find out exactly what you need to do to bring your purpose into alignment with their purpose.

Once you know precisely what they want you to do, you can then select the message which best harmonizes your purpose and their purpose for the speech.

PULLING IT ALL TOGETHER INTO A CLEARLY TARGETED MESSAGE

Perhaps you have noticed that I use the term *message* a great deal in this chapter, while in previous chapters I have more frequently used the word *speech*. There is a good reason for that: The two are not just different words for the same thing.

The best way to explain the difference may be to think of a speech as if it were a truck, and the message as if it were the payload which the truck carries.

You're already ahead of me, aren't you? I realize it is quite possible to give a speech with no message. In fact, making a speech without giving a clearly targeted message is probably the most frequent mistake the average speaker makes. Perhaps that is one major reason so few people really look forward to sitting through a typical speech.

Even more important, the practice of giving speeches without messages is what keeps most speakers from having a strong impact upon their audiences. High-impact speakers always consider their own purpose for speaking and their audience's purpose for listening; then they pull it all together into a clearly targeted message.

Defining Your Message

Impact comes from having and delivering a message that is clearly defined, sharply focused, and easy to remember.

Think for a moment of how some of the great speakers of history have done that. The central message of Franklin D. Roosevelt's famous fireside chats can be characterized by one quote: "We have nothing to fear but fear, itself." John F. Kennedy's potent inaugural address is best remembered by the sentence: "Ask not what your country can do for you; ask what you can do for your country." They had a way of pulling it all together into a simple, very memorable statement or phrase.

Other great speakers use mnemonic symbols, an acronym or a few words which help you to grasp quickly and remember what they have to say. Dr. Robert Schuller probably is the best example of this technique in the world today. He will often take a word like "love" and let each letter in it carry a part of his message: "Live, Others, Vision, Enthusiasm;" that's what LOVE is all about!" he'll say.

But before you can come up with a phrase or symbol for your message, you must get that message focused very clearly in your own mind. You must define your central unifying thought into a message you can deliver with impact.

What that basically means is that you narrow down all the wonderful things you want to say into a single short sentence which says it all. Since that takes a lot of creative energy and self-discipline, let's look first at what targeting can do for you. Then we'll look at how to do it.

What Targeting Can Do For You

Targeting your message includes selecting a subject based on your purpose and the purpose of the audience, and deciding what clearly focused idea you want to get across as your message.

To get a clearer picture of what targeting can do for you, let's look more closely at what the television networks expect of the "main titles" we mentioned in an earlier chapter. They are among the most targeted messages being sent today.

The networks expect them to:

1. grab attention immediately and hold it
2. introduce the subject to be covered in the show
3. set the tone, pace, and mood for the show
4. introduce the characters and convince the audience that they are good people to spend time with—people you can identify with
5. compel you to do what they want you to do
6. dispel any fears you have about watching the show

In a very real way, this is what you must accomplish to get the response you desire from your audience.

Five basic strategies are required for you to target your message for maximum effect, regardless of what type of speech you are making.

Strategy 1: Target Your Purpose

The most important consideration in choosing your message is: What do you wish your audience to do in response to your communication? For example, do you want the audience to laugh, to cry, to feel better about themselves, to feel like trying harder, to understand something new, or to agree to something? You might want them to do several or all of those things, but unless one of them dominates, it will be a confused audience when you finish.

Have mercy on your audience; know what you want them to do and tell them. Don't leave them guessing what they, according to you, should be doing.

Strategy 2: Target Vital Subjects

People listen to speeches for one overriding reason: they are seeking to satisfy certain needs or desires. If people had no unsatisfied needs or desires, they would never come to hear you speak. What the people in your audience want may be nothing more than to be entertained, or to have their curiosity satisfied, or it may be that they are attending because they are required to and want to keep their jobs.

If needs and desires are the reason people listen to speakers, your strongest message is the needs or desires felt most keenly by your audience, and ways they can satisfy them. The better you understand the needs and desires of your audience members, individually and collectively, the more impact you will have when you speak.

However, it is not enough to merely understand what your audience wants; you must make that the target of your message. Address a person's need in a way that indicates hope of meeting that need, and you immediately get that person's attention. Convince the person that the action you propose will satisfy that need, without ignoring other needs, and you get the action you desire.

Strategy 3: Target Subjects You Know Something About

Nobody likes to hear a person rattle on about a subject which he or she knows little or nothing about. If you want to speak with impact, stick to what you know best. Your audience impact rating goes up in direct proportion to your knowledge of a subject.

I am often invited to speak to audiences on subjects about which I know little or nothing. Unless the proposed subject is one that I can easily find out enough to talk intelligently about, I usually suggest another topic, recommend a fellow speaker, or decline the invitation. I respect both my audience and my career too much to run all over the country showing my ignorance.

There is also another good reason for sticking to subjects you know something about; they usually reflect your interest. You will always have more impact when you are speaking about subjects in which you have a vital interest.

Strategy 4: Target Ideas That Are Manageable

A beginning speaker often seeks to cover the entire history of the world in a five-minute speech, but the experienced speaker knows there is a limit to what an audience can grasp, and what a speaker can effectively present, in a given time.

Have you wondered why most local newspapers refuse to run a picture of more than three or four persons, and prefer only one person? The reason is simple: the eye can only focus on limited images. Crowd twenty-five people into a single picture, and each person becomes so small that you cannot recognize anyone.

Ideas for speakers are like that. Try to cover too many ideas, and they all seem to run together. Your audience will become so confused no one can understand what you are talking about. For example, if you are speaking to request that your company be put on the approved bid list, stick to that request. Be brief, be specific about what you are asking, and be direct in your approach to it. When you present too many requests, each of which requires some consideration, you stand a good chance of getting nothing done.

Few of us can fire "the shot heard round the world," or change the pattern of history, or correct all the abuses we see by giving one short speech. It's better to chip away, a little bit at a time, with many small and precisely targeted messages.

Strategy 5: Target Ideas That Are Easy To Remember

It may come as quite a shock to you, but several weeks after the speech is over people in your audience will not remember what you said, but they will remember how they felt.

If you try to remember all the wonderful things said by the most recent speaker you've heard, you will see that it's true. If you are like most people, you will not even be able to remember the main points. You might remember a story you particularly enjoyed, or a funny line you liked, but not the main points the speaker worked so hard to get across. However, if that speaker made a real impact upon you, chances are good you will at least remember the central, unifying idea—the message—of his or her speech.

If that's true, why not make it as easy as possible for people in your audience to grasp and remember the one predominant message you want to get across? To do that, you must choose the appropriate message, clearly focus it in your own mind, and deliver it with the appropriate impact. Then, and only then, can you expect your audience to give you the response you desire, and to remember your purpose for making the speech.

SO, WHAT HAVE WE SAID?

If you want people to act, to do something, to buy something, or to understand important information, you must take a results-oriented approach by:

1. knowing specifically what you want to accomplish
2. making your message fit your audience's purpose
3. pulling it all together into a clearly targeted message.

ACTION STEPS

1. Reflect on a speech you have given in which you were not completely satisfied with the results. In light of this chapter, analyze how you might have gotten better results.

2. Select an upcoming (or imaginary) speech and decide how you will accomplish each of the three things suggested in the chapter summary.

8 HOW TO PREPARE A POWERFUL SPEECH

PURPOSE

Your speech is the vehicle for delivering your central thought, or message. Although we have talked mostly about how to gain favor and create interest, all that favor and interest will not do you much good unless you have something worthwhile to say and can say it with impact.

Together, let's explore:

1. how to gather the materials you need
2. how to prepare your speech for maximum impact
3. how to plan for a powerful close

> "I use not only all the brains I have, but all I can borrow."
> —*Woodrow Wilson*

SAYING WHAT YOU WANT TO SAY WITH IMPACT

Most books on public speaking advise first sifting through countless books and articles to learn as much as you can about a subject before you decide what to say. As you discovered in the previous chapter, my method is to do precisely the opposite: to decide what you want to say, then look for all the supportive information you can find to add power to it. There are several reasons for this.

First, if you do not know a great deal about a subject, it is a waste of your time and creative energies to speak about it. Besides, showing your ignorance will do nothing to endear you to your audience.

Second, to speak with authority, you have to believe yourself, and the only way you can have confidence in what you are saying is to know precisely what you want to say. If you do not know and believe your message, then neither will your audience.

Third, never underestimate your audience. If you simply memorize and parrot a collection of other people's ideas, the audience will see right through you. Once you know your message (your central unifying thought), you are then ready to start adding power to your presentation of that message.

GATHERING ALL THE MATERIALS YOU NEED

There is a big difference in knowing your message and knowing all there is to know about it. You may know clearly the central unifying point you want to get across, but it is always wise to:

1. check your knowledge and beliefs against the latest information on a subject
2. look for supporting materials which can help you explain and prove your message

The more you know about a subject, the more forcefully you can present your case. Obviously, the more complex your speech, the more research you need to do. Let's look at some productive steps to gathering materials.

Step 1: Get Your Facts Straight

"Obviously, a man's judgment cannot be better than the information on which he has based it,"[1] said Arthur Hays Sulzberger.

---

[1] Arthur Hays Sulzberger, quoted by Arnold "Nick" Carter in *Communicate Effectively*, (Gretna, LA: Pelican, 1978), p. 93. Copyright 1978 by Arnold Carter.

Nothing weakens an attempt to convey a message as much as faulty information. This is especially important if you are criticizing someone or taking a radical stand on an issue. All your audience has to do is to catch you in one factual error, and the credibility of your entire speech is damaged. Make sure you know what you are talking about. Never assume; check!

Step 2: Look For Supporting Data

Next, gather all the data you need to make a strong case for your central message. Collect quotes, specific examples, research data, and anything else that will support or clarify your position. Gather more than you plan to use so you can select the strongest items of information.

"I quote others only the better to express myself," said Montaigne. It's a great idea to quote a leading authority in your subject area. For example, giving your opinion about a certain aspect of stress management would not be nearly so powerful as citing the findings of a recent research project by Harvard Medical School.

Look for all the supporting data you can find. The more of it you have available, the greater the impact of your speech.

Step 3: Study Your Materials Carefully

It is also important to prepare by studying the materials you have gathered. You will be surprised how much your confidence increases as you learn more about what you are attempting to communicate.

Something else happens when you really get into studying the materials you have gathered: You begin to get enthusiastic about your subject. And the more enthusiastic you are, the more convincing you will be when you speak.

Step 4: Make Notes

"The palest ink is greater than the strongest memory," said an ancient Chinese wise man. When you come across a great piece of supporting data, or a quote which adds a lot of punch, write it down. If you don't, either you will later have to waste a lot of valuable time looking for it, or you will remember it right after you have delivered your speech.

There is also another good reason for writing things down. It helps you immensely in selecting and organizing the materials you will actually use. I have found it helpful to use small index cards on which I write the quote, or a summary of the data, and the source.

That way, I can shuffle through cards to find things, which is much easier than shuffling through books and magazines.

Step 5: Select The Materials You Will Use

Obviously, you cannot use all the data and quotes you have collected, especially if you've done a good job of research. "The secret of being a bore is to tell everything," according to the great French philosopher Voltaire.

If you cannot use all the material, why go to the trouble of gathering it? That's a good question, and I will use an analogy as an answer. The pressure of water at a tap is directly proportional to how much water is in the tank which supplies it; the more water in the tank, the greater the power where you need to use it. It is the same with information. The more of it you start with, the greater will be the power of the information you will use and the points you will make.

Pare all your information down by choosing the two or three points most likely to get the response you desire. In other words, look for the information that is most likely to get people to act as you wish them to act.

Once you have selected your main points, look for the materials and arguments that present them in the clearest light and support them most emphatically. Choose the images and explanations that best explain any part of the point that needs clarification for your audience.

Do not assume the audience understands everything you understand. What you know very well, they may not know at all. So define your terms, explain your conclusions, and guide them to understand what you have discovered.

Select information, materials, and arguments that add the most credibility to your main point. If you know your audience, you can select the supportive materials they will find most convincing. Keep paring it all down until only the essential points, ideas, arguments, and supportive data remain.

Step 6: Let It Age

Most messages, like fine wines, improve with age. For example, it has been reliably reported that Abraham Lincoln allowed his "House Divided Against Itself" speech to ripen in his mind for thirty days before delivering it. Spouting out half-baked ideas and expressions make muddled speeches which often produce a response opposite to what you desire.

Often, when I have an important speech to prepare, I dictate a rough draft. Then I let it ripen for several days, during which time I question everything I have said. If it is really important, I test my statements on people whose judgments I value. Once I feel that I have really digested what I want to say, I will then dictate a final draft. This process has helped me to avoid the consequences of making some bad mistakes in speaking.

ORGANIZING YOUR SPEECH FOR MAXIMUM IMPACT

"Brevity is the best recommendation of speech, whether in a senator or an orator," according to Marcus Tullius Cicero.

Being brief is crucial to speaking with great impact, but brevity is not simply cutting something out when you realize you are running out of time. Brevity is something you should build into every point and statement you wish to make. It is a matter of organizing and presenting your points in the briefest way possible for the impact you want.

"Brevity is not a virtue; it is a result. In a word, if you would be brief, first be long," said Charles W. Ferguson in *Think* magazine.[2]

What we are really talking about is planning what you will say. Here are some pointers on how to do just that.

Pointer 1: Organize Your Message

Every speech you make will have more impact if you organize it to accomplish precisely what you desire. When you first try this, you might find it a laborious task. However, once you develop the habit of organizing, it becomes second nature to you.

In the previous chapter, we saw how vital it is to boil your message down into one succinct statement, one central unifying thought. We also discovered that the message should be clearly targeted, simple to understand, and easy to remember.

It is not unusual for a skilled speaker to spend more time organizing the central message for maximum simplicity and impact than he or she spends on all the other parts of the speech combined. Such speakers know that the central message is the foundation upon which everything else rests.

---

[2] Charles W. Ferguson in Eleanor Doan, *The New Speaker's Sourcebook* (Grand Rapids, MI: Zondervan, 1968), p. 56.

Pointer 2: Organize Everything Around Your Central Message

Haven't you noticed that what makes the punch line of a joke funny is that it has been carefully set up by the telling of a story? In other words, the punch line is the whole reason for telling the story. Few punch lines are funny when said alone.

Likewise, your central message has more impact when everything you say sets it up. That does not mean that your message should always be the last line of a speech, as the punch line is in a joke. It means the whole speech should be organized so that the central message is presented in the most powerful way.

It might be helpful to think of your speech as a display, like a department store window. Every accent in a good window display is there for one purpose: to call attention to the merchandise to be sold. In a good sentence, or a good song, or a good commercial, every component exists and is arranged to call attention to its most compelling point.

This approach might sound restrictive to you at first, but as you experiment with it you will find it holds a wide range of possibilities. For example, you can set up the message as the opening statement and use the remainder of the communication to explain and support it. Or you can repeat the central message again and again throughout the speech, using supportive materials to set it up each time you use it. Or you can use the novelist's approach and build suspense until you are ready to spring the message. Whatever your technique, your goal is to display that central message to maximum advantage.

Pointer 3: Build A Strong Introduction

A strong speech always has at least three major components: an introduction, a main body, and a closing. When you understand the purpose of each, you can use them together as a skilled artist uses paint brushes to create a finished picture.

Let me pause to clarify the difference between the content introduction and other introductions I have mentioned.

First, I explained the need for a strong written introduction which would present you to the audience, and which would be read by someone else. Its purpose is to tell the audience why they should listen to you and to help you gain favor with the audience.

Second, I explained how important your opening remarks and actions are in selling yourself to the audience. This kind of introduction enables you to introduce yourself to the audience in the most favorable way.

Both of those introductions, or openings, are vital to your success in speaking.

The introduction we are now talking about, however, is designed to announce the subject you will be speaking about. Its primary purpose is to draw people into what you are about to tell them.

Notice, for example, how local television stations do it with teasers for their newscasts. A "newsbrief" might say: "Fire sweeps through a downtown hotel killing seven people...details at eleven." Now, that's a real grabber! It grabs you because it does more than get your attention. It creates interest in what the station is about to tell you. It draws you into the newscast by alerting you that what will follow is important to you. It is, therefore, a good introduction.

Poor speakers fail to use introductions to good advantage because they depend on them only to attract attention. I am sure you have heard speakers say something like, "Sex! Now that I have your attention, I want to talk to you about... ." That approach might attract attention, but it does nothing to draw the audience into the speaker's subject.

A good introduction must always convince an audience that what is about to be said is something they should hear.

Pointer 4: Develop A Strong Main Body

The main body of your speech serves to present the message in the clearest and most powerful way. A good main body does four things:

1. It entertains by making the message interesting.
2. It instructs or informs by clarifying what you have to say.
3. It persuades by convincing the audience that what you say is true.
4. It motivates by inspiring people to act as you wish them to act.

While each of these four functions is vital in its own right, they should not be separated from each other, but should be carefully interwoven throughout the entire main body. If, for example, you start out with strong humor, it is seldom productive to shift to a professorial approach. Audiences are fickle; as soon as the fun is over, they tune you out. If you use humor, a strong form of entertainment, it should be sprinkled throughout the entire presentation.

The most convenient way to organize the main body of the communication is to use three basic points. You might start out with the central message as your first point, and then use a second point to explain it and a third point to convince the audience to act in relation to it. Or you can use the first two points to set it up, then present the unique selling proposition as the third point. Use your imagination and try several possible arrangements before you commit to a final outline, but always present the central message in its most convincing setting.

Pointer 5: Develop A Good Outline

You might find it helpful to think of your introduction, main body, and closing as a skeleton on which you can hang all your information, ideas, arguments, and explanations. The analogy can help you to give your speech structure and shape. It can also help you keep the various parts in perspective, and help you remember what you are going to say.

The head, or introduction, is the nerve center and primary sensing area. It contains mechanisms for seeing, hearing, tasting, feeling, and smelling. And it contains the brain, which sends signals to every part of the body. A good introduction alerts as many of those senses as possible that something exciting is about to happen.

The main body contains the digestive system, the center of the emotions (at least symbolically), and the connecting links for the appendages. Thus, the main body of the communication fulfills the promise of the introduction. It provides the substance of the hope excited by the introduction, gives a solid anchor for the embellishment of the appendages, and gives impetus to the legs and feet to carry out the desired action.

You might think of the closing as the legs and feet, which carry all the weight of what you have said. It is the task of the closing to make the audience give you the response you desire.

Because I consider the closing so important, however, I want to treat it separately in this chapter. But first, let's look at one more vital element of preparing a powerful speech.

Pointer 6: Write Out Your Speech

It is always a good idea to write out your speech as a final stage of preparation. That might strike you as a strange statement, since I have strongly suggested you not read your speech. However, there are several good reasons for writing it out.

First, it helps you crystallize your ideas and sharpen your expressions. Even if you speak in a very conversational tone and, therefore, write in a conversational tone, you will find yourself saying more, in fewer words, and with greater impact.

Second, it aids you in practicing what you will say. By having a written text, you can more easily pick up the flow of ideas, reinforce the location of your illustrations, and work on your transitions between points.

Third, writing it out helps you to build in brevity while you time the speech. As you go along, you will find yourself looking for ways to cut out superfluous remarks and to shorten everything you say. If you read the whole speech and discover it takes you an hour longer than you have to speak, you know instantly that you must do some cutting. It is far better to cut your speech while you can still use scissors than to wait until you are on your feet and rapidly running out of time.

Fourth, writing out your speech gives you a permanent written record of what you have said. If you make many speeches, this could save you a great deal of time. Instead of writing a whole new speech, you can often adapt parts of what you have already used.

In short, you'll be miles ahead (and so will your audience) if you write out your speech and practice it thoroughly before you give it.

That brings us to the all-important closing.

PLANNING FOR A POWERFUL CLOSE

Except for the first minute you stand before an audience, the last minute of your speech is the most crucial to your impact as a speaker.

What most speakers overlook is that speaking is basically an emotional experience rather than an intellectual process. Two weeks after you've spoken, people will not remember all the wonderful things you said; you are lucky if they remember your central message. However, they *will* remember how they felt as you drew your speech to a close. They will remember if you touched them where they lived, or if you simply quit talking. That's why I always hate to hear a speaker talk furiously right up to the last minute, then say something like "Well I see my time is all gone...bye."

I cannot emphasize enough that your closing must be planned even more carefully then the rest of your speech. It is the only way you can assure that it will give your speech the impact it deserves.

Let me share some tested and proven techniques which always enable me to close with power.

Closing Technique 1: Quit While You Are Ahead

There are only two "unforgivable sins" a speaker can make. The first is to bore your audience, and the second is to speak longer than your allotted time. The second one is, by far, the least forgivable. Yet speaking too long is one of the most common mistakes public speakers make. It's easy to do. If you really get into what you are saying and feel a rapport with the audience, it is hard not to lose track of time. "Time flies when you're having fun!"

If your message matters to you as much as it should, you may assume that everyone present feels the way you do. That is a dangerous assumption to make because it is almost never true, and it is the surest way to kill whatever enthusiasm the audience has for your ideas.

The only safeguard against this tendency to run over is to plan to close on time, then close according to your plan. That planning starts with the introduction and runs through every phase of your speech.

One good tactic for planning to close on time is the segmenting approach television talk show producers use. They know up front exactly how much time they have to work with and allocate this time by segments. They decide in advance how much time each segment should take; then they monitor carefully to see that none gets more than its allotted share. If, for example, the first segment runs thirty seconds over, they know they have to cut thirty seconds off another segment. By constantly adjusting the time, they can finish right on schedule.

Obviously, you cannot use a stop watch to keep track of how much time you have left, but you can use the basic idea. You simply decide in advance how much time your introduction will take and allot it that much time. Then you allot time for each of your three major points. Then all you have to do is monitor your progress. If you run over on one point, that time will have to come off of another one, or it will come off of the closing.

Most important, you need to know precisely how much time it will take you to give a good solid close, and stop—wherever you may be—when you come to that point.

Like many of the tactics I suggest, this one will feel stilted and awkward to you the first few times you use it. But as you practice it more and more, you will find it to be a lifesaver to your reputation as a high-impact speaker.

Closing Technique 2: Go Out With A Bang

Since the audience will remember more of how they felt than of what has been said, I usually close with a powerful story. It is the best way I have found to go out with a bang.

In fact, I have even been able to salvage a few disastrous speeches by using a strong close. If I had to make a choice, I would always rather have the audience in the palm of my hand at the close than at the beginning.

To give you a great send-off, a story must do several key things. First, it must grab the audience. It can be an inspiring story about human triumph in the face of overwhelming odds, or a funny story everyone can identify with, or a short story with a powerful punch line.

Second, it must be short and develop quickly. Most of my closing stories run less than one minute.

Third, it must be related to your message. It is even better if it can pull together everything you have said and reinforce your central message. A particularly powerful closing ends with a strong punch line which summarizes your central message. You can repeat it a couple of times, then just let it hang in the air.

Fourth, it must be a story you can tell very well. I can tell sports stories all day because of my background as a coach, but sports stories might be hard for a musician or a history professor to pull off. Stick to what you can do best, and practice doing it until it becomes an art with you.

While I strongly recommend the closing story approach to going out with a bang, there are other approaches you can use effectively. You can, for example, briefly summarize the main points you have made. Put the whole speech into two or three short but memorable sentences and repeat them a couple of times, with special emphasis on the central message.

What is important is that you find a closing that works well for you, and keep practicing it until you can always go out with a bang.

Closing Technique 3: Give Them Something To Do

A good closing puts legs to the whole process of speaking. It carries the audience into the response you desire.

That response might be a standing ovation, or it might be giving you an order, or it might be taking some action you have outlined. Whatever it is, a good conclusion invites people to act as you wish them to act. To accomplish this, the closing must explain very clearly and precisely what action you desire and be very convincing in its tone.

It all comes down to knowing what you want and working throughout your whole speech to get it. But the job is not finished until you wrap it up and take it home.

Make sure, however, that your audience is inspired to do what you want them to do. Michigan's famous football coach, "Hurry-Up" Yost, once inspired his team with the conclusion of his half-time pep talk to such a high level that they followed him out the wrong door—right into the swimming pool.

Closing Technique 4: Give Them Something To Remember

Good speakers always leave an audience with something to remember. You might leave them with a challenging question, a glowing promise, or a strong statement of your central message. Mostly, though, they will remember how they felt. So always leave them feeling good toward you.

SO, WHAT HAVE WE SAID?

In this chapter we have seen that your speech is the vehicle you use to deliver your central thought or message. It does little good to work hard gaining favor and creating interest unless you have something worthwhile to say and can say it with impact.

To make sure you always do that, you must:
1. gather the materials you need
2. prepare and organize your speech for maximum impact
3. plan for a powerful close.

ACTION STEPS

1. Think about the most powerful speech closing you have ever heard and analyze what made it so powerful.
2. Plan at least three strategies for implementing what you have read in this chapter in your own public speaking.

9 HOW TO PRESENT YOUR IDEAS WITH MORE POWER

PURPOSE

In most business presentations and speeches, impact translates into power—the ability to get people to act. Those who can convey their thoughts and ideas with power are usually the ones who get ahead in almost every career field.

To enable you to do that, let's explore:

1. how to make your audience understand what you mean
2. how to make them care enough to act

> "Boasters by nature
> are from truth aloof."
>
> —*Geoffrey Chaucer*

POWER COMES FROM CLARITY AND PERSUASION

In order for people to act the way you want them to act, they must first understand what you mean by what you say. Then they have to care.

A statement like "Present economic conditions necessitate the utmost austerity in acquisitions for the foreseeable future," will probably leave most people confused, at best. At worst it is not likely to get much action.

However, if you say "We're in a bad slump right now, but if we watch our money very carefully for the next six months we might all be able to hang onto our jobs," that gets the point across with both clarity and persuasion.

High-impact speakers take full responsibility for making people understand and care. They know that saying "They misunderstood what I meant" is only a statement of the problem—not a solution. They also know that it is their task to motivate people, to make them want to act.

Let's look at how to approach these two all-important tasks.

HOW TO MAKE YOUR AUDIENCE UNDERSTAND WHAT YOU MEAN

Sol Linowitz, former chairman of the Xerox Corporation, once served as ambassador to the Organization of American States, where confusion is often a problem. Mr. Linowitz told of a meeting with a group of Central American presidents, when one head of state politely asked about his old company.

"I explained what the company did, and my interpreter translated into Spanish," Mr. Linowitz said. "The group, obviously awestruck, looked at me with new interest and respect, and began talking with one another in great animation and apparent incredulity."

"Concerned, I asked the interpreter to tell me exactly what he had told them. He replied, 'I told them just what you said—that Xerox is a company that has invented a new method of reproduction'."

In that case, the problem grew out of the language barriers between people who were trying to communicate with each other. Unfortunately, the same problem often occurs among people who supposedly speak the same language.

Here are some tools you can use to speak with greater clarity.

Clarity Tool 1: Use Straight Talk

The novice speaker tries to impress everyone with big words, complex sentences, and complicated explanations. The skillful speaker knows that people are much more likely to understand straight talk.

It might be far more flattering to your ego to throw out a smoke screen that shows you are "smarter than everyone else," but it will not get you what you want—understanding.

Instead of cultivating a vocabulary of big, vague, and seldom-used words, let me urge you to develop a good vocabulary based on straight talk.

Straight talk is made up of simple, strong, and active words that mean exactly what they say. It also uses short and simple sentences that are easy to follow. It is a language almost anyone can understand.

To get a better idea of how it works, check out these word comparisons.

abhor—hate
aid—help
anecdote—joke
avid—eager
challenge—dare
commence—begin
container—bag, bottle
demise—death
elderly—old
exchange—swap
firearm—gun
futile—hopeless
humorous—funny
manufacture—make
notion—idea
obstinate—stubborn
perspiration—sweat
error—mistake
educational institution—school

accelerate—speed up
allow—let
anticipate—expect
beneficial—good for
combat—fight
concerning—about
courageous—brave
donate—give
excessive—too much
fatigued—tired
for—because
garment—dress, suit
inform—tell
mentor—teacher
observed—seen
peril—danger
dine—eat
exhibit—show

In each case, the words on the left are good words, but the

words on the right say things much more clearly and with greater impact.

If you want your audience to understand you, learn to use straight talk.

Clarity Tool 2: Use Vivid Images

Using vivid images enables your audience to clearly understand your message and meanings. Notice the vivid imagery in the following line from William Shakespeare's *Richard III:* "Lord, Lord! me-thought, what pain it was to drown." You can almost feel the agony of the character in that image.

Vivid imagery is easier to illustrate than it is to explain. For example, see how vivid the images are in the following definition of anatomy by a very small boy:

> "Your head is kind of round and hard, and your brains are in it. Your hair is on it. Your face is the front of your head where you eat and make faces. Your neck is what keeps your head out of your collar. It is hard to keep clean... Your stummick is something that if you don't eat enough it hurts, and spinach don't help none. Your spine is a long bone in your back that keeps you from folding up. Your back is always behind you no matter how quick you turn around. Your arms you have to have to pitch with and so you can reach the butter. Your fingers stick out of your hand so you can throw a curve and add up rithmetic. Your legs is what if you have not got two of you can't get to first base. Your feet are what you run on; your toes are what always get stubbed. And that's all there is to you except what's inside and I never saw it."

While you can't say much for his grammar, and it would be hard to prove medically some of the functions he cites, it gives you a vivid picture of a human body—as he sees it.

If you would be clear in your expressions, learn to use vivid—not flowery or ornate, but vivid—images.

Clarity Tool 3: Use Short, Punchy Stories

Studies persistently show that people remember stories more than they do anything else, after they have heard a speech. Therefore, clever public speakers always use many stories in every speech they give. I know some top professionals who spend much more time preparing their stories than they do the rest of their speech. Let's look at some key reasons that short, punchy stories help so much in clarifying your ideas.

First, stories give your audience a point of identity. A well-chosen story often makes members of your audience understand how an idea relates to them. And remember, identification is the key to all effective communication. When something becomes personal, it becomes very interesting. Stories can help your audience connect.

Second, people like good stories and tend to listen more closely to them. Notice, for example, how quiet everything gets when you start telling a story. There's a little child in all of us who loves to hear stories.

Third, good stories help people to grasp complex ideas. They are like windows which let in light on the subject. In fact, sometimes you can make your point with a good story even though you never come out and say it in plain words.

Fourth, stories reinforce memory. Often, when someone remembers a good story you have told, they will also remember the point you made in telling the story.

So, let me tell you a story about a famous American and notice how it does all four of the things I have outlined.

> He was born in Columbus, Ohio, 1890, the third of eight children. At eleven he quit school to help with the family expenses, and got his first full time job at $3.50 a week.
>
> At fifteen he became interested in automobiles and went to work in a garage at $4.50 a week. He subscribed to a correspondence home study course on automobiles. Night after night, following long days at the garage, he worked at the kitchen table by lamplight.
>
> His next step was a job with Frayer-Miller Automobile Company of Columbus. One day when he felt ready, he walked into the plant. Finally Frayer noticed him.
>
> "Well," he said, "what do you want?"
>
> "I just thought I'd tell you I'm coming to work here tomorrow morning," the boy replied.
>
> "Oh! Who hired you?"
>
> "Nobody yet, but I'll be on the job in the morning. If I'm not worth anything you can fire me."
>
> Early the next morning the young man returned to the garage. Noticing the floor was thick with metal shavings and accumulated dirt and grease the boy got a broom and shovel and set to work cleaning the place.
>
> That man was Eddie Rickenbacker, who went on to gain a national reputation as a race car driver and automotive expert. In World War I he was America's leading Ace. Later he founded Eastern Airlines.

As you can see, that story says all that needs to be said about what it takes to get ahead in the world. It's got determination written all over it.

If you want to see your impact take a quantum leap, invest a lot of time in learning how to tell short, punchy stories.

Clarity Tool 4: Cultivate Good Grammar

Good grammar is a must for consistently making people understand what you mean. Grammar is the set of rules which govern the use of the language. While I would never argue that you should become rigid in obeying the rules, I would suggest good grammar can almost always help you make things clearer.

Your words become *you* to your audience. They convey a strong message about your professionalism and attention to detail. Some speakers would not consider wearing sloppy clothes or shabby shoes while speaking; yet they think nothing of murdering the "King's English."

Grammatical errors can become so ingrained in us that we are not even aware of how often we make them. Here are some tips from *Education Reporter* to help you avoid some of the more common mistakes people make when speaking:

- Don't use no double negatives.
- Make each pronoun agree with their antecedent.
- Join clauses good like a conjunction should.
- Verbs has to agree with their subject.
- Just between you and I, case is important, too.
- Don't use commas, which are not necessary.
- Try to not ever split infinitives.
- Its important to use apostrophe's correctly.
- Proofread your writing to see if any words out.
- Correct spelling is esential.

Some audiences might identify with you better if you use slang and colloquial expressions, but more often than not you will make a bad impression. Good grammar helps you make your meanings much clearer.

Clarity Tool 5: Use Visuals

Have you ever wondered why so many speakers use a lot of visual aids in business presentations and speeches? It's simple—they work!

We have already discussed using slides, overhead projectors, and other visuals. However, there is one type of visual aid that deserves special attention because it can help so much in your efforts to gain clarity and have all your meanings understood. It's the ever-popular flip chart, and it's dynamite with small groups.

The following pointers on using flip charts offer some good advice to anyone who wishes to speak with greater impact.

FLIP CHARTS CAN LIVEN UP YOUR PRESENTATIONS

Flip charts can liven up your presentations to small groups and enable you to reinforce points easily and effectively. Yet many speakers are hesitant to use them because they do not know how, and others use them poorly.

Flip charts offer some strong benefits:

Visual Impact   More than 80 percent of what we learn comes through our eyes.
High Interest   People will watch with great interest while a speaker writes or draws almost anything.
Authority   Your main points look much more impressive when you write them down, especially numbers.
Reinforcement   Nothing provides a more convenient review than flip charts.

Tips On Better Flip Charting

Here are some tips which can help you become more effective at using flip charts.

1. *Become professional at it.* If you are a professional speaker or an expert consultant, don't use a flip chart like an amateur. Here are some ideas for improving your chart-side manner.

    a. *Practice.* Practice using a flip chart until you are totally at ease with it. You don't want to always be striking over words, or running out of room, or fumbling with the pages. You want your audience to be completely comfortable with the flip chart.
    b. *Be prepared.* Always start with a new pack or pad so you will never run out during a presentation. Make sure the easel is sturdy and the pad is firmly attached; test all markers before you start, and have everything you need at your fingertips.
    c. *Focus on your audience.* You are there to talk to people—not the chart. Learn to draw from the side without turning your back to the audience, and never talk into the flip chart.

d. *Don't apologize for not being a commercial artist.* That's not the reason you were invited to speak. The less you say about your writing or drawing skills, the less they will be noticed by your audience.

2. *Focus on clarity.* While you do not have to be a graphics expert to use flip charts effectively, it is helpful to become good enough to have your words and illustrations clearly understood. Here are some pointers to help you do that.

   a. *Use a large pad.* Always use the largest size pad you can take with you on an airplane, or obtain locally. And unless you are a graphics expert, stick to white paper.
   b. *Use wide-tipped markers.* Narrow tips produce fine lines which (even though they might look neater) are hard to read from a distance.
   c. *Use colors.* Black with red or blue will enable you to accent more details.
   d. *Write legibly.* Most lettering on a flip chart should be at least 1 1/2 inches tall—2 or 3 inches is better. Print or write so that every letter can be read easily.
   e. *Watch spelling.* When you misspell a word, it hangs there as a sign shouting out "MISTAKE!"
   f. *Letter horizontally.* Vertical or slanted writing is hard for some people to read.
   g. *Emphasize.* Make the salient points jump out. For example, if you predraw a chart in black, underline the important features in red as you present it.
   h. *Keep it simple and uncluttered.* Avoid complicated shading or other methods of indicating dimension or depth. It's the symbols that count, not the realism.

3. *Avoid distractions.* Flip charts can help you gain and hold attention, but they also contain some potential distractions of their own. Here are some ways to avoid those distractions.

   a. *Avoid blank pages.* Write something on the first page of your flip chart (a greeting, benefits you can offer, or a clever saying) to avoid having clients stare at a blank page while you're getting ready to use the chart.
   b. *Avoid inactive illustrations.* During the presentation, finish each sheet as quickly as possible, then remove it so it won't distract after it has served its purpose.
   c. *Avoid playing with markers.* It's almost impossible to hold a marker in your hand without playing with it. Put it down when you are not using it.
   d. *Don't use a pointer.* Gesturing with your hand is much better. However, if you feel you must use a pointer, make sure you point it at the chart—not at your audience.

e. *Don't doodle.* It's easy for a flip chart to become a great big scratch pad on which you doodle. Unless you make every mark count for you, it will count against you.

4   *Customize your presentation.* Flip charts offer a great way to customize presentations so that the client feels it is tailored to his or her interest. Here are some ways you can do that:

   a. *Use the client's name.* It is a good idea to write in advance the name of the client at the top of each page.
   b. *Personalize visuals.* Avoid the impression that your presentation is a "traveling show" which is too general to be of interest. Use visuals that relate to the specific client.
   c. *Destroy the chart as you go along.* Carry some masking tape, tear off important sheets, and stick them around on the walls. Make sure that your client feels the flip chart you've used was for his or her eyes alone.
   d. *Write responses.* As you get feedback from your audience, write down key words of that response so they will feel involved.

By following these simple guidelines, you can master flip charting. You will find it to be a valuable aid in helping people understand what you mean by what you say, every time you speak.

Now, let's look at the second important aspect of speaking with greater impact—making people care.

HOW TO MAKE PEOPLE CARE ENOUGH TO ACT

It matters little if people understand everything you say if they do not care enough to give you the response you desire.

I like the story about the poll-taker who asked a man if he agreed that one of America's greatest problems is public apathy. "I don't know, and don't really care," the fellow said flatly.

But you want people to care. In fact, you want them to care enough to act on whatever message you give and whatever requests you make. Let's look at some strategies for making people care enough to give you the response you desire.

Care Strategy 1: Be Sincere

"I will not say that I am loyal or that Your Majesty is gracious," Alfred Tennyson once wrote to Queen Victoria, "for those are terms used or abused by every courtier, but I will say that during our conversation I felt the touch of that true friendship that binds human hearts together whether they be kings or cobblers."

Nobody likes false flattery, but everybody likes sincere compliments like the one described.

One of the first things I learned on the speaking circuit is that people can spot a phony a mile away. They will warmly receive you if you will come to them sincerely and always be completely honest with them. Moreover, they will care about what matters to you if you show that you care what matters to them.

Care Strategy 2: Be Convincing

The most convincing statement in the English language begins, "What's in it for you is. . . ." Remember, people do things for their reasons, not for yours or mine.

1. *Sell your ideas.* Your task as a speaker is to convince your audience to buy your ideas—not just to inform them. Review your speech to make sure it conveys a value that makes the audience want to do what you want them to do.
2. *Make it warm and personable.* Does your speech "smile"? Does it present you as a likeable person?
3. *Make it credible.* Avoid unsupported superlatives like "most exciting idea in America," or "best product in its field." Make sure readers will readily accept all your claims. If not, provide strong documentation for each claim.
4. *Make it complete.* Make sure your speech contains all the information an audience will need to decide in your favor.

To really make people care, you have to be very convincing.

Care Strategy 3: Be Enthusiastic

"Nothing great was ever achieved without enthusiasm," said Ralph Waldo Emerson. I agree wholeheartedly. Your audience will never become any more enthusiastic than you are about your ideas. If you believe in what you are saying, make them believe it!

Dale Carnegie probably did more to elevate the art of public speaking in America than any other individual. One of his favorite tactics was to stop a speaker in mid-speech with a startling question.

"Do you believe what you are saying?" he would ask.

"Certainly I believe it!" the novice speaker would reply.

"Then make me believe it !" Mr. Carnegie would challenge.

The best way you can make anyone believe what you have to say is to become completely enthusiastic about it.

SO, WHAT HAVE WE SAID?

Two of the most urgent tasks you face in making business presentations and speeches are to make people understand you and to make them care enough to act on your ideas and requests. That's what impact is all about—it's your ability to get people to act.

If you can convey your thoughts and ideas with power you can more often get the action you desire.

ACTION STEPS

1. Think about a time when a speaker enabled you to see a complex idea quite clearly, and analyze how he or she did it.

2. Plan some strategies of your own, based on this chapter, for improving your batting average at making people understand and care what you have to say.

10 GETTING WHAT YOU CAME AFTER

PURPOSE

How will you know how well you've done if you don't have a way of keeping score? In this chapter, we will discover how to know whether you've gotten the desired response by:

1. getting good feedback throughout the speech
2. getting useful feedback after the speech
3. evaluating to make sure your next speech is your best one

> "When you say that you agree to a thing in principle you mean that you have not the slightest intention of carrying it out."
>
> *—Otto Von Bismarck*

HOW GOOD ARE YOU, REALLY?

The story is told of a super salesman who sold an incredibly efficient filing system to a certain business concern. A few months later he dropped by the office of the company to check up on its operation.

"How is the system working?" he inquired eagerly.
"Beyond our wildest dreams," the manager replied.
"And how's business?" the salesman asked.
The manager smiled, "We had to give up our business in order to run the filing system."

Two kinds of success concern the high-impact speaker—short- and long-range success. Short-range success has to do with the audience's understanding and receiving the actual presentation. Long-range success has to do with the ultimate effect the speaker desires. Both are important.

If you want to make sure you always get both long- and short-range success, you need two kinds of feedback: presentation feedback and message feedback. Presentation feedback tells you if your audience heard and understood what you presented. Message feedback tells you if they gave the response you desired.

Let's look at some ways you can get both presentation and message feedback.

HOW TO GET GOOD FEEDBACK DURING YOUR SPEECH

One of the things I suggest people do is to develop a sixth sense for looking at the nonverbals that come from your audience. In that way you will be able to pick up any signs of boredom, confusion, or open hostility.

Another technique I use is very common to selling. It is called the *trial close,* and it works by periodically asking questions like "How does this look to you? Does this look like the kind of thing that might be interesting? How does it sound so far? What is your reaction to this?"

As long as I get a positive feedback from the audience, I know that I am on the right track.

HOW TO GET USEFUL FEEDBACK AFTER THE SPEECH

Sophocles wrote tragedies to the very end of his long life. Because of his zeal for writing he seemed to be neglecting his business affairs, so his sons summoned him to court and asked a jury to pronounce him incompetent to manage his estate on the grounds of senility.

Then the old man is said to have recited to his judges a play which he had just finished, *Oedipus at Colonnus,* and to have asked whether the poem seemed the work of a man in his dotage. After his recitation, he was freed by a vote of the jurors.

That's useful message feedback!

Here are some ways you can track your results through good feedback.

Plan Your Feedback Before You Make Your Speech

How will you know if the audience does exactly what you want them to do? That question can help a great deal if asked before you make the presentation.

It might help you discover that the presentation you have planned does not have the power to give you the response you desire. You can either develop a more powerful presentation or adjust your expectations to be more realistic. Or you might discover that portions of the presentation are weak in relation to the response you hope to get, and you can make adjustments to strengthen them. It is always better to spot weaknesses in presentations before they are given than to be disappointed later.

STRATEGIES FOR GETTING FEEDBACK

Several strategies have been developed by skilled speakers over many years and have proven successful in getting the feedback you require.

Strategy 1: Test Your Message—Not The Audience

High-impact speakers always assume the responsibility for communicating. Only an amateur blames the audience for a failure, except in rare instances.

The best test of your effectiveness as a speaker is how much of your presentation your audience understood and how close they came to the response you desired. However, that has more to do with your presentation and message than with how good an audience it was.

Strategy 2: Test Your Effectiveness— Not Your Abilities

Fishing for compliments is not useful feedback. Asking people questions like, "Did you enjoy the presentation?" might produce glowing tributes, but it will not tell you anything useful. Specific questions that reveal what that audience understood you to say, and how they related to what you said, can be far more productive.

Strategy 3: Ask Questions, Listen, And Observe

Careful listening and observation can often tell you more about how effective a presentation was than a formal approach reveals.

A local television talk show host once told me how he knew it was a hit, long before the ratings proved it. "When I was doing another show, people would come up to me and tell me they'd seen the show and enjoyed it. But after the first few shows in this new series people would stop me on the street to give me their opinions about the subjects we'd been discussing. There's all the difference in the world in the two kinds of response," he said.

If someone compliments you, draw them out with questions to see if what they understood is what you meant. Observe the kinds of responses people give you.

Strategy 4: Give the Audience Something To Do Immediately

Make sure they understood that you are not evaluating them, but that you are interested in their opinions. "I've been telling you what I think, now I'd like to hear what you think about this subject," is a good way of introducing your request for feedback.

Strategy 5: Fit Feedback To Your Goals

A speech might produce an immediate effect that is desirable, but might result in a long-range problem for you. For example, you might sell an idea to one group of coworkers, but in so doing, you might alienate another group that is equally vital to reaching your long-range goals. Or an idea that thrills top management might be strongly resisted by the middle management people who will have to help you implement it.

Strategy 6: Follow Up On Feedback

If you are not going to do anything with feedback, why bother getting it? Feedback only has value when it is put to good use.

Good follow-up requires more than a casual glance through a few of the questionnaires your audience returns. In fact, doing nothing about feedback can sometimes produce negative results. A supervisor who tells employees, "We want your input on management decisions," and then never does anything about the suggestions they make can expect those workers to question his or her sincerity.

If feedback indicates that your message has been received, make sure you follow through to take advantage of all of the success. You might be tempted to think of a good presentation as an end within itself, especially if it has taken a lot of work to put it together. However, a successful presentation is often only the beginning.

If, for example, your feedback indicates that you have staged a successful meeting which has produced some strong decisions, follow up to make sure those decisions are implemented. Or if your short-range feedback indicates that your audience has heard and understood you, make sure that you follow through to ensure that they give you the long-range response you desire.

When a group responds positively to your presentation, don't simply pat yourself on the back and walk away. Take advantage of the opportunity to build future successes. On the other hand, if your feedback indicates that your presentation was not as successful as you would have liked, take advantage of that feedback to learn how to do it better next time.

HOW ALWAYS TO MAKE YOUR NEXT SPEECH YOUR BEST ONE

"Experience," says Aldous Huxley, "is not what happens to a man; it is what a man does with what happens to him."[1]

A novice gloats in a success and learns nothing useful from it. The more experience you gain as a speaker, the less you are concerned with praise. The real question becomes, "What works best for me?"

It's like when I take my automobile to a mechanic. He puts it

---

[1] From Charles L. Wallis, *A Treasury of Sermon Illustrations* (Nashville: Abingdon Press, 1950). Copyright 1950 by Pierce and Smith.

on a diagnostic machine that tells him instantly what needs to be done to tune the car for maximum performance. His concern is not "Does it run?" but "How does it run best?"

As a speaker, I am equally concerned with what works best for me in every situation. I listen and analyze my feedback so that I can fine tune every speech to its maximum effectiveness. My goal is not just to be good at what I do, but to be superb at it.

Likewise, the novice crawls off from a failure and says, "I really blew it this time!" But the high-impact speaker asks, "Where did I go wrong?" He or she wants to know what to do differently next time to ensure success. Through careful listening to feedback, you can correct your mistakes and do a better job next time.

Here is a useful list of questions you can ask to critique each speech.

- Was I sharp? (prepared? alert? organized? enthusiastic? funny?)
- Was my delivery of professional quality? (entertaining? informational?)
- Was my audience involved? (interested? empathetic? excited?)
- Would the audience and meeting planner like to have me speak again?
- Did I take advantage of all the opportunities this engagement offered me?

As a professional speaker I use speech and seminar evaluations. In this way I am able to find out things that often prove helpful. Mostly, I look for criticism. I know that I can do 400 speeches and achieve 99 percent excellence but I am more in tune with those things that are wrong, and I am a much better speaker for it.

For example, one of the problems that showed up in my evaluations was a bright red tie I had been wearing. I had no idea that it was unattractive until I read the seminar evaluations and discovered that tie was a major turn-off to quite a few people. You can be sure that I immediately ditched that tie.

SO, WHAT HAVE WE SAID?

The only way you will know when your audience does what you want them to do is to find out through carefully designed feedback. Good feedback does more than stroke your ego; it tells you how successful you have been in accomplishing your goals, in what way you have been successful, and what works and does not work. Feedback can tell you if you have obtained results, both in the short and long range.

However, feedback only has value when you carefully analyze what it means and follow up on it. You can use it to take full advantage of your success, to build future successes, to correct mistakes, to tell you what works best for you, and to fine tune your communications skills.

It's what I call making the score—making sure you got what you came after.

IT IS RESULTS THAT COUNT

One of the worst feelings in the world is to give what you consider an earth-shaking speech, only to have the audience sit there like so many bumps on a log. Getting results is *always* the name of the game in public speaking, whether those results are measured in laughs, tears, commitments, or actions.

Let's briefly review the F.I.T.S. formula for high impact public speaking:

F stands for gaining Favor—selling yourself.
I stands for creating Interest—getting their ears.
T stands for conveying a Thought—sending a message.
S stands for making the Score—getting what you want.

Put them all together and you've got a speech that F.I.T.S. your occasion, your audience, your purpose, and your style, the kind of speech that gets results.

IF I MAY SAY IN CLOSING...

Arthur Rubinstein, in the final years of his life, was asked by a television reporter, "Do you have any regrets?"

The world-famous pianist, who was nearing his death at age ninety-five, thought for a moment, then replied "I'm ashamed to say this at the end of my life—which is now, but there are many pieces I was never able to perform for an audience because I was too lazy to practice enough to do them well."

Like the great Rubinstein, most of us are too lazy to become the best we could become. The key to success is the sweat of practice. Yet sometimes we can learn from the successes and failures of people who have gone before us and who willingly have shared what they have learned. I wrote this book to help you shortcut some of the things that I and many others have learned through years of experience and practice.

Only you can determine how good you will become as a speaker. I hope the ideas and insights I have shared with you will help you to get off to a great start toward becoming a high impact public speaker.

INDEX

INDEX

INDEX

A

Animation in presentation, 64
Audience:
  awareness of, 59
  control of, 35-37, 52
  distraction of, 71-79
  feedback from, 120-23
  holding, 56-66
  identifying with, 37-38, 61-62, 111
  involvement with, 37-38, 63
  making friends with, 25-26
  in opening of speech, 30
  reading your own, 32-33
  sensitivity toward, 58
  targeted message and, 85-87
  understanding, 59-62, 87-88

B

Bad verbal habits, 70
Benson, Dr. Herbert, 24
Breathing, 24-25
Brevity of speech, 99

C

"Care" strategies, 115-16
Cassette recorder, use of, 11
Charisma, x
Clarity:
  in flip chart use, 114
  as source of power, 108
Closing of speech, 100, 103-6
Communication and role of identification in, 111
Control of audience, 35-37
Control pointers for stage fright, 22-26
Conveying a thought, xiii-xiv, 91-92, 108-17
Convincing, being, 116
Creating interest, xiii-xiv, 57-62
Criticism, constructive, 10-13
Critique of one's own speech, 124

D

Delivery, 42-53
Diction, 47-48
Disasters, avoiding, 69-73

Distraction(s):
  of audience, 71-79
  environmental, 74-77
  in use of flip charts, 114-15
Dress, 34

E

Enthusiastic, being, 116
Environmental distractions, 74-77
Equipment problems, 75-76
Exceeding allotted time, 4, 104
Experience as aid to public speaking, 2-6, 13

F

F.I.T.S. formula, xiii-xiv, 56, 125
Faulty information, avoidance of, 97
Favor of audience, gaining, xiii-xiv, 56
Feedback, 2-3, 120-23
Flip charts, use of, 113-15

G

Gaining favor of audience, xiii-xiv, 56
Gathering materials, 96-99
Grammar, 48, 112

H

Hecklers, handling, 78
Holding interest of audience, 68-79
Humor, uses of, 9-10, 23-24, 50-51
  in handling interruptions, 78-79
  as ice breaker, 35

I

Ice barrier, breaking with humor, 35
Ideas:
  creating interest in, 57
  presenting with power, 108-17
  targeted, 85-92
Identification with audience, 37-38, 61-62, 111
Images, vivid, use of, 110
Impact of speech, xi-xiv, 39, 42-53, 60-61, 99-106, 108-17
Information, faulty, 97

Interest:
　creating, xiii-xiv, 57-62
　holding, 68-79
Interruptions:
　of audience, 71-79
　environmental, 74-77
Introduction of speaker, 32
Introduction of speech, building, 100-101
Inviter, point of view of, 87

J

Jargon, 60

L

Location of speech, 74

M

Main body of speech, 100-102
Message, clearly targeted, 86, 88-92
Movements and facial expressions, 7, 13, 34, 51-52

N

Non-verbal communication, 33-34, 51-52
Notes, 97-98

O

Objectives of speech, 84-85, 90
Opening of speech, 30-40
Organization of speech, 99-106
Outline of speech, 102
Overreacting to interruptions and distractions, 77

P

Pacing, 49
Pauses, 49
Peale, Dr. Norman Vincent, 9, 45, 47, 73
Personality and manner, 25-26, 33-34
Persuasion, as source of power, 108
Physical involvement with audience, 63
Planning to prevent problems, 69
Platform techniques, 44-53
Practice, 6-13
Public speaking:
　animation in, 64
　audience and, 30, 37-38, 56-66, 71-79, 85-87, 120-23
　bad verbal habits, 70
　breathing, 24-25
　brevity, 99
　closing, 100, 103-6
　control, taking, 35-37
　control of stage fright, 22-26
　conveying a thought, xiii-xiv, 91-92, 108-17
　convincing, being, 116
　creating interest, xiii-xiv, 57-62
　criticism, constructive, 10-13
　critique of one's own speech, 124
　delivery, 42-53
　diction, 47-48
　disasters, avoiding, 69-73
　distractions, 71-77
　dress, 34
　enthusiastic, being, 116
　environment of, 74-77
　experience as aid to, 2-6, 13
　F.I.T.S. formula, xiii-xiv, 56, 125
　feedback, 2-3, 120-23
　flip charts, 113-15
　gaining favor of audience, xiii-xiv, 25-26
　gathering materials, 96-99
　grammar, 112
　holding interest, 68-79
　humor, uses of, 9-10, 23, 35, 50-51, 78-79
　"ice barrier", 35
　ideas, conveying, xiii-xiv, 91-92, 108-17
　identification with audience as key, 37-38, 61-62, 111
　images, use of, 110
　impact of, xi-xiv, 39, 42-53, 60-61, 99-106, 108-17
　introduction, building a strong, 100-101

Public speaking *(cont.)*
  introduction of speaker, 32
  inviter, point of view of, 87
  involving audience, 63-65
  location of speech, 74
  main body of, 100-102
  message, clearly targeted, 86-92
  movements and facial expressions, 7
  non-verbal communication, 7, 33-34, 51-52
  notes, use of, 97-98
  objectives of speech, 84-85, 90
  opening of, 30-40
  organizing, 99-106
  outline for, 102
  overreacting to interruptions, 77
  pacing, 49
  pauses, 49
  personality and manner, 25-26, 33-34
  platform techniques, 44-53
  practice, 6-13
  "prime time" part of speech, 82
  problem prevention, 69
  reading a speech, 70-71
  relaxation techniques, 24-25
  response factor, 57-58, 62-65
  rhythm patterns, 49
  self-confidence, 25
  sincere, being, 115-16
  speed of delivery, 49
  stage fright, 16-27
  stories, use of, 8-9, 105, 110-12
  straight talk, 109-10
  stress in, 17-18
  style, developing your own, 4
  subjects, 90-91
  time limit, exceeding, 4, 104
  time pressures, 21
  visuals, 53, 64-65, 112-15
  vocalizing tips, 8
  vocal power, 47-48
  voice, 6-8, 48
  "What's In It For Me?", 103
  writing out speech, 102-3

R

Reading a speech, 70-71
Reading your audience, 32-33
Relaxation techniques, 24-25
Response factor, 57-58, 62-65
Rhythm patterns, 49

S

Schuller, Dr. Robert, 46, 51-52
Self-confidence, 25
Sensitivity to your audience, 58
Seyle, Dr. Hans, 17-18
Sincere, being, 115-16
Speaker, introduction of, 32
Speed, varying in delivery, 49
Stage fright, 16-27
Stage presence, 43-46
Stories, use of, 8-9, 105, 110-12
Straight talk, 109-10
Strategies for feedback, 12-23
Strategies for targeting message, 90-92
Stress, as source of stage fright, 17-18
Style, developing one's own, 4
Subjects, 90-91
Symptoms of stage fright, 18

T

Targeted ideas, 91-92
Techniques for platform use, 44-53
Thought, conveying, xiii-xiv, 91-92, 108-17
Time:
  exceeding allotted, 4, 104
  pressures, 21
Tips for involving audience, 63
Tips on use of visuals, 65
Toastmasters, 11
Tone of voice, 48
Trial close, use of, 120

U

Understanding your audience, 59-62

V

Verbal habits, bad, 70
Videotape camera, use of, 11-12

Visual distractions, 76
Visuals, use of, 52-53, 64-65, 112-15
Vocabulary. *See* Straight talk
Vocalizing tips, 8
Vocal power, 47-48
Voice, 6-8, 48
Volume of voice, 48

W

"WII-FM" or "What's In It For Me?", 103
Word usage, 60, 109-10
Writing out speech, 102-3